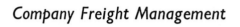

Company Freight Management

Company
Freight
Management

Introduction to cost-effective freight transport
with guide to the Transport Act

George Allan Hughes

Gower Press

First published in Great Britain by Gower Press Limited
140 Great Portland Street, London W1N 5TA
1969

Set in 11 on 13 point Times and printed by
Hazell Watson & Viney Ltd
Aylesbury, Bucks

Contents

CONTENTS

Illustrations

Introduction

We live in a time of rapid change. Perhaps this is more true of the transport industry than of any other industry. Technical books on transport rapidly become out of date. Most people administering or otherwise involved in the transport of freight or passengers therefore tend to amass piles of technical journals or to tuck away any scraps of notes which appear relevant to their particular problems. As the years go by these notes and journals turn up at the edges and go yellow.

Such piles and "scrap" files will never be eliminated, so this book is certainly not an attempt to replace them. It is rather an attempt to focus attention on those areas demanding major decisions, to isolate the most important factors which influence decisions and to analyse some ways in which practical solutions may be achieved. It is written with the following types of transport executive in mind:

1   The practitioner who has long been immersed in technicalities of transport operation.
2   The newcomer to fleet operations.
3   The newly styled "distribution controller" or "director" who wishes to begin to understand those complexities which members of his traffic department refer to in conversation with him.
4   The student of transport who wishes to prepare himself for a career in transport management.
5   The managing director or board member or potential managing director who senses something wrong with the transport side of the business but

is without adequate understanding of the problem
and therefore is unaware of what to do next, or at
what point to attack the problem.

It is hoped that this is a book which may be read now and also
dipped into later. The occasional frivolity it contains is in no
way meant to detract from the importance of the message it is
designed to impart. This is that the movement of raw materials
or semi-finished products onto the production belt and the
distribution of the finished product are too frequently regarded
as a cost "burden" that can be neither avoided nor minimised.

To keep this book to a manageable size discussion of the
operation of warehouses has been excluded, even though this is
often an important aspect of transport manager's responsibilities. Also excluded are also the problems of packaging and
goods and materials handling which beset those operating a
transport organisation. These are both subjects worthy of a
book in themselves. This book will examine the problems of the
carriage of goods when normally considered outside the control
of the factory staff and therefore unfortunately sometimes
considered uncontrollable. This is in a sense definable as
when the goods are on the other side of the factory gates.
Depot and stocks are considered only in so far as they would
affect this transportation problem.

It is surprising how often high costs are passively accepted.
Transport can and should be subject to the same financial
disciplines as other parts of a business. The success of all the
techniques employed and all the skilled effort put into the job
can only properly be demonstrated in financial assessments
made in statements as akin to "profit and loss" accounts and
balance sheets as possible. Transport is a service. But the value
of the service provided must be measured against the costs of
producing this service.

The introduction to scientific management techniques is
intended to demonstrate what may be achieved. There will
always be a place in the management of a service for the "rule
of thumb" practitioners. Decisions do have to be taken quickly,

for there is little opportunity in day to day management to stop and think. But satisfactory management also involves long-term planning. It is in this that scientific techniques are of benefit, provided always that the application is made with an understanding of the nature of the transport service to be provided. It is often more advantageous to teach a transport man the simplest new management techniques and let him use them with an understanding of their limitations than to bring a management services specialist into transport to apply his techniques with zeal but without an essential understanding of the nature of the problem.

For many years now it has not been unusual for the transport manager to be considered the mere servant of the managers of other departments and not as a competent member of the team directing the business. This is changing. The transport manager needs to be able to:

1   Plan and control complicated distribution and input transport operations.

2   Manage men who are by character independent and encouraged to be so by the nature of their occupation.

3   Demonstrate and use the specialised knowledge which is required as handling systems and packaging grow more sophisticated.

4   Appreciate the problems of vehicle engineering and maintenance.

5   Embody enough business good sense to deal with carriers both large and small who provide a variety of services in order that satisfactory deals are made to cover the provision of such services.

To do all these jobs well requires a talent and management ability and a quality of leadership which are rarely found even in candidates for the most senior posts. Unfortunately the transport manager in the larger companies may also have to succeed in the "business politics." These are often entirely unrelated to transport efficiency but involve attendance at company social functions, membership of the right associations and behaviour in public and sometimes even in private which demonstrates acceptance of the company myth that it is a team working harmoniously toward specific acceptable objectives. A happy ideal—but seldom achieved.

Managers in transport will soon have to prove they have other talents in order to qualify for the licence or certificate of transport management which will be required of them. An instinct to do the right thing is no longer enough. Knowledge must now be demonstrable and therefore formalised.

It is hoped that the following pages will provoke thought. They may also clarify some much debated issues. They may help the transport manager to present his case more easily to the licensing or certifying officers of the future and the directors that have always been there. The unfortunate connotations of certification in the past might become all the more applicable to the increasingly twisted and perverted transport scene. Good intent, diligence, and safe practice are no longer enough to ensure success.

ONE

Analysing the company's exact transport requirements

It is not often that the transport manager can start "clean." Usually improvements have to be made to an existing situation which is considered unsatisfactory. Situations most often become unsatisfactory as the result of:

1 A rapid growth in the business.
2 Changed marketing techniques or practices.
3 A growing awareness of inefficiency in a cost-conscious business climate.
4 An awareness of the advantages of transport or distribution specialisation.

The fact that a system suited to a relatively small business is no longer appropriate for a much larger volume of business takes a surprisingly long time to be recognised. This not only applies to management of a private fleet of vehicles but also to arrangements with carriers. A distribution system which is economically efficient for one marketing pattern becomes, not surprisingly, inefficient if the number of points to which deliveries have to be made are altered or the average consignment size or package weight changes. The tendency towards the "test marketing" of products in different areas imposes a temporary strain on the

1

transport operation. Although the principles of scientific management were largely developed as the result of analysis of production, the growing cost-consciousness in business does not stop at the end of the production belt. The importance of the whole distribution operation and the significance in this operation of the part played by transport have made transport an obvious target for attempts to increase efficiency. New vehicles designed to allow more intensive use of the equipment are streaming onto the market.

The need therefore is for a periodic reappraisal of the situation. When the working day of the transport manager is occupied continuously in keeping a delicately balanced transport operation in progress, to find time for reappraisal is not always easy. The transport manager may also be prejudiced. For example, it is possible to pay too high a price for reliability of service. But it does make the transport manager's life easier. If the cry is constantly for a better service there may be a temptation to buy one, but it can be very expensive to move from a reasonably reliable service to one providing a first-class service on demand.

The alternative to paying for superb service may be to spend a lot of time and effort anticipating and eliminating possible failure. This will undoubtedly mean a need to increase the "stand-by" facilities available. If, however, the cost of planning and the extra facilities do not exceed the high price to be paid for a superbly reliable service then obviously they should be provided to the net advantage of the firm. An objective appraisal would show this, whereas a subjective appraisal (especially if it is one conducted by a tired transport manager who has recently had to explain delivery failures or a shortfall in supply) may not.

Even company directors have been known to take into account their own personal comfort when making a decision which is likely to make this short-lived. It may therefore be useful to use consultants. Because of the nature of the problem, however, if consultants are used they should be consultants experienced in transport. Transport does tend to be an emotional topic.

2

Because operations are open to inspection and everyone is affected directly or indirectly there are dangers that those who live with the job of movement become submerged in well-meant and not so well-meant criticism. Most transport men would welcome the opportunity to solve problems together with someone who knows the business, for transport managers lead a lonely life.

Transport services

The demands for service result in the provision of quite different sorts of operations. For the purpose of this book the transport which the transport manager controls may be divided into three groups, as follows:

Incoming freight

The movement of raw materials or semi-finished products which usually form inputs to factories were most often originally planned as short-distance movements. More and more frequently, however, they have become quite extensive operations because of the change in the location of supply of the raw material or semi-finished product.

Alternatively, the location of the manufacturing unit might have shifted due to a firm's rationalisation.

Examples of distance movements of raw materials are those of china clay, sometimes of sand, and there are considerable movements of semi-finished steel and car shells. The characteristic of this type of transport operation is that the consignments are large and provide bulk and often regular movement. The commodities themselves are often of low value and this has therefore traditionally reflected itself in low rail rates. As rail rates initially set the pattern for road rates, especially in the conveyance of bulk materials, this has meant low charges to the user. Because of the nature of the product and the character of the movement, it is usually possible to exercise firm control over the operation.

3

Delivery to wholesalers or stockists

This is usually a less substantial movement than that of raw materials or semi-finished products. Despite this, consignments are still largely organised in vehicle or part-vehicle loads whether by rail or by road. The probabilities of a closely controlled and well-disciplined operation are still possible but less probable than in the case of raw materials.

(Movement of raw materials or of finished products typify the inter-factory movements which may be considered an extension of the production line.)

Distribution of goods to customers

Distribution either from factory or from stores to shops or direct to customers usually involves conveyance of comparatively small units. There is inherent in this business a demand for rapid, safe, and reliable service. The goods transported are often susceptible to theft and to damage. Often the movements must be made over wide areas of territory and frequently involve distribution all over the country.

There is a growing incentive for firms, even when competing with each other in marketing products, to join together to gain the benefits of a greater throughput for a national or widespread distribution system. It is in this field, too, that carriers, providing specialised or general services in limited areas or operating more extensively, are developing and apparently making money. It is in this area that British Rail, who are still the principal carriers in this country of small consignments both by passenger and by goods train, has long been vacillating between developing or withdrawing from the business.

Overseas movements require different consideration to goods transported in the United Kingdom. Trunk movements tend to be longer, the documents required for customers, carriers, and customs are complicated and both packaging and insurance considerations differ. The requirements of overseas customers or producers are not easily generalised, so this aspect of the

4

transport problem is not considered. There are specialist books on the subject and there will be more.

Marketing and sales department requirements

It is unnecessary to enter into an esoteric discussion about the difference between marketing and selling. As far as a transport manager is concerned, they are the same. They are the originators of the demand for a distribution service. It is from the salesmen and the market research organisation that the firm takes its data about consumer preference and the way in which the product should be designed and presented. This includes both the design of the goods itself and the packaging. There is then a demand for the following.

Immediate delivery

In practice "immediate" delivery often turns out to be *reliable* delivery within a *reasonable* time. The time which is acceptable for the delivery of goods varies with their nature. A firm which produces stoves and boilers is probably reasonably happy with an interval between receipt of order and delivery of about two weeks. A chain store, on the other hand, with a "rapid" turnover in many urban stores with very small reception storage areas will require delivery within hours. A mail order store would probably be content with delivery in two or three days of receipt of an order but if it could at modest cost speed delivery to within one or two days it would gain a sales advantage over its competitors. Where retail stores are supplied, a product needs shelf space. It is likely that should a shop run out of stock the shelf space will be taken by another product. From the salesman's point of view the position then has to be re-established. The product has again to be displayed and to be made available on demand. One of the facts of business life which the transport manager grows to accept very quickly is that salesmen tend to use the transport service as an excuse for their own occasional inefficiency. They are not always to be blamed for this, especially when the firm happens to distribute in that area through a carrier.

In a highly competitive situation it is important for the salesman to maintain in the customer's mind the image of his own firm's efficiency and reliability. To rely upon continuing orders this is essential. It has almost become traditional that when a customer expresses dissatisfaction at the failure to meet difficult delivery dates the firm should claim that the goods have already been dispatched. This is easiest when the goods are sold ex works. More and more, however, goods are not sold ex works but are sold delivered. In such circumstances whether or not the goods are carried in one's own vehicle is immaterial. The customer is entitled to expect the firm to choose the most appropriate means of carriage whether this is in public carriers' vehicles or in privately owned vehicles.

It is perhaps wisest for the transport manager to accept the difficulties which face the salesman. When failure to meet delivery dates recurs, of course, it is important that the subsequent necessary investigation is conducted by all the departments involved. A decision should be taken as to whether the fault lies in the ordering, production, stock control, or in the transmission of the orders.

Acceptable costs

The marketing organisation includes in the unit price structure for the product an element for transport if the price is "delivered." Even where the product is not sold delivered the product is frequently offered in conjunction with a delivery service, for which a separate charge is made. The unit for sale is almost always much smaller than the transport unit concerned. It is comparatively easy for a large load such as an atomic flask to be charged for in a way which is realistic and appropriate. Where there are large numbers of small packages, however, as is frequently the case with consumer goods, then the allocation of a unit delivery cost is difficult. It is less so, perhaps, where a carrier is used and a scale of charges exists relevant to the average package size.

Where distribution is made in one's own vehicles to a large number of places through the country, it is necessary to average costs. This can cause cross-subsidisation which involves further problems, to be discussed later. There exists, too, the possibility of discounts for bulk delivery or for acceptance in off-peak periods. Inclusion of an appropriate price for transport in a delivered selling price is, however, sometimes made difficult by long-standing practices and traditions in a particular trade.

For example, it is often very difficult to deliver pharmaceutical goods to district nurses, doctors or welfare clinics, but the suggestion of higher-than-average charges would make life very difficult for the salesman. Nurses, doctors, and clinics introduce the product to the consumer who thereafter tends to buy through chemists or at supermarkets.

Presentation to the consumer in good order

It is demanded that the product tendered to the customer be in a brand new condition. If this is not possible then the sale clearly was not made in good faith. All too frequently minor damage or deterioration in perishable goods is the cause of poor customer relations which in the end manifest themselves in reduced trade. Offer of replacement is not satisfactory. The time spent in sorting out and in correspondence on claims can cost firms a great deal of money in addition to a deterioration in customer relationships.

In a modern affluent society the value of goods carried is often high in relation to their bulk. As the products are frequently mass produced and are therefore not readily identifiable one from the other, then they are often easy to dispose of after theft. Loss of a full vehicle load of a high value product could seriously affect the trading position of a medium sized firm. One of the worst manifestations of this kind of poor service is the practice of some carriers who accept no responsibility for anything other than wilful misconduct on the part of their staff. They claim to have effected delivery by the tender of the wrappings of a package, the contents of which have been stolen.

Capacity to absorb peaks

The need to cater for "peak" forwardings, which are created by increases in seasonal demands for the products or which are the results of promotional schemes, is obvious. If these peaks are substantially higher than the normal level of forwardings, this causes the transport requirement to be higher at only very limited times of the year. If it is necessary to convey the product in privately owned vehicles or the peak happens to occur at a time when transport is in great demand, such as in the pre-Christmas period, this may necessitate provision of vehicles for use on only a few occasions a year, producing a serious cost problem. The whole question may be exacerbated by the fact that it is at such peak periods that congestion occurs in acceptance of goods by customers. At the very time, therefore, that vehicles are needed for the movement of goods to customers, the delay at customers' premises can become excessive.

Provision of an order-taking service

Not only in some distribution systems must the vehicle drivers be of a disposition and character which preserve the goodwill of the recipients of the product, but in some cases drivers are also required to act as order takers, if not indeed as salesmen. Where the sales force is merely used to establish initial contact with the customer and to make sure from time to time that the goodwill of the customer is maintained, the vehicle driver might be responsible for ensuring and collecting a regular repetitive order. Even if this is not so, cheerful co-operation and compliance with reasonable requests in the placing of goods at the recipients' premises often retains a customer who might otherwise turn for satisfaction elsewhere.

Production department requirements

Supply on demand

The raw material input to the production process or the movement of semi-finished goods or of manufactured goods into warehouses may be regarded by the production manager as a service to his activity. Because design of the product and manufacture are often the reason for the existence of the firm it is frequently essential for the transport services before, and sometimes during, the productive process to be geared to production. The often small extra costs involved and the disciplines of long-term planning of production in conjunction with the transport operation are sometimes rejected, but more usually disregarded without proper appreciation of the cost reductions possible if the whole operation is planned together. The high cost of interrupting a regular productive process, or varying the batch throughput in a productive process, is not always justified by lower costs in transport. Recognition, however, is growing that the net return from an investment can be materially affected by overall long-term planning of the business from the procurement of the raw materials to the effective delivery of the finished product.

Rapid inter-factory movement

The transport fleet is sometimes used, where firms have premises in different places, as an extension of the conveyor belt or production line. Transport on demand is often again requested because detailed analysis of the manufacturing operations is not always extended to the transport part of the operation. It is significant when a method study is undertaken that the symbol for transport recurs frequently in flow diagrams. Where large movements are concerned, as in the case of some major motor car assembly firms where car shells are moved from one part of the country to another for completion, suitable disciplines are advantageous and are introduced.

Minimum deterioration of the product

Just as, in the distribution operation, the product must be presented to the customer in an acceptable condition, so, in the productive process, there are minimum standards for the product condition. Certain grades of steel must be protected from condensation. Bananas must be moved in a time which

9

does not permit them to over-ripen. Short distance movement of molten metal at Scunthorpe must be achieved without an excessive temperature drop. This is a condition which often applies to chemicals when moved in insulated tanks. Because these are movements in bulk it is usually easier to exercise the degree of control necessary. It is less easy when a distribution service is provided.

Instant removal from the end of the production line

The firm's policy on stock-holding sometimes throws a burden on to transport. Goods are rarely allowed to accumulate at the end of the production line. They must be moved to warehouses or stock-holding areas. When a fast selling line turns into a slow moving one this can sometimes mean the shifting of the product from place to place until sales are again matching production output.

Financial department requirements

Minimum cost

Although both the sales and production departments in a cost-conscious enterprise will not make demands without being aware of the financial implications of these demands, the imposition of cost disciplines is the prime responsibility of the financial department. These financial disciplines will not only cover the cost of operations of vehicles and equipment, they will also include the financial liabilities of working capital tied up in the goods being moved. This, of course, becomes more important as markets become more extensive and goods in movement, or awaiting movement, increase.

Production of control statistics

Not only are financial disciplines imposed upon the transport department by the financial department, but transport must also contribute its share in the production of the criteria against which success or failure is measured. This almost inevitably will include participation in the formulation of budget forecasts and in the determination of standards.

General management requirements

Minimal effect on net profit

There is a growing awareness among general managers of the effect of transport on the net revenue of an enterprise. This varies of course with the nature of the product. Where the product is of high unit value, despite the difficulties of transportation and the need for safety during transportation, the proportion of total cost and of total selling price represented by transport are usually less than if the product is of low value. As the criterion of the value of the goods carried now tends to be less significant in the compilation of carriers' charges than it used to be, this is re-emphasised.

Satisfactory public image

It is general management and board members, more often than sales managers and marketing executives, who insist on the expensive liveries of some vehicle fleets. It is hard to quantify the value to the firm of hand-painted bodywork. If the livery preserves the corporate image on which successful trading has developed, then it may be worth a great deal. As the fashion turns to simple streamlined efficiency, however, then a self-coloured simple livery, which is often cheap, is probably as effective as a more elaborate one. The public image required of transport by general management also includes road safety and vehicle cleanliness. Both these features of themselves contribute to greater efficiency and would in any case be regarded as part of the transport manager's own minimum requirement.

Travel agency service

Strangely, but not infrequently, the general management requires a busy transport manager not only to operate a fleet of vehicles, to deal with carriers, to solve efficiently and quickly the many problems which arise on the periphery of his

11

activities in connection with packing or warehousing or storage, to arrange the provision of company cars, but also to fix reservations in trains and aeroplanes and also in hotels, when members of the board or senior executives travel. This can divert a transport manager's attention from those problems which he alone can solve.

The services which are required of a transport manager are therefore extensive. Despite this he is rarely judged on the economic efficiency with which he produces these services. This is not to suggest that he is not judged by absence of complaints or by the results of occasional inspection, but that he rarely faces the financial and economic tests which are frequently applied to others. Often the major factor in the determination of the seniority of a transport manager is the overall value of the goods transported or the expenditure on transport. The transport manager's position may simply be decided by the number of vehicles he controls or the size of his staff.

Summary of chapter

1   The transport manager needs to reappraise his problems from time to time.
2   Because of the nature of job he may find transport consultants' services helpful.
3   The cost of a superb service must be compared to the effect and cost of a less efficient but cheaper service.
4   Input of raw materials to factories or movement to wholesalers or stockists are usually more easily controllable than distribution services.
5   The marketing and sales department require:
   (a) Reliable delivery in reasonable time.
   (b) Transport at a cost which does not make impossible continuation of good selling practices.
   (c) Presentation of the product in good order.
   (d) Reasonable service at times of greatest demand.
   (e) Cheerful co-operation to maintain customer good-will.

6 The production department requires:
  (a) Supply on a demand which is planned to reduce the firm's costs and not just the production department's costs.
  (b) Rapid inter-factory movement in situations where transport has become in effect part of the production belt.
  (c) Minimum deterioration of the product.
  (d) Removal from the end of the production belt and the holding of stocks.
7 The financial department requires:
  (a) Financial discipline.
  (b) Production of control statistics.
8 The general management require:
  (a) Minimal effect from transport on the net return of the firm.
  (b) Production of a satisfactory public image.
  (c) Many ancillary services.
9 The transport manager is rarely judged on the economic efficiency with which he produces what is required of him.

TWO

Organisation for accurate costing

The economist is tempted to describe costs in terms of alternatives. The cost of a television receiver is that which has to be gone without to have the set. This could be a summer holiday or a new carpet or a number of visits to the cinema. The cost of having a new articulated vehicle could be doing without an extension to a depot, a larger loading bay at the distribution warehouse, a more convenient storage arrangement or an even more luxurious carpet and the services of a glamorous new secretary. Such measurements in uncommon denominators are inconvenient. For practical purposes it is difficult to quantify a motor vehicle in terms of glamorous young secretaries, even though it might be fun to try. The young ladies might resent being traded for inanimate objects. It is convenient, therefore, for costs to be assessed in monetary terms, but it is unlikely that money will be stocked for its own sake, so cost really does depend on a choice between things.

The following factors must usually be taken into account when deciding on costs:

1   Estimated expenditure to maintain and operate the equipment.
2   Provision for replacement of the equipment.
3   Allowance for the capital invested.

Obviously the equipment will have to be maintained. Equally it is obvious that there are operating costs. If a fleet of vehicles is not being run down, from time to time the units have to be replaced. Whether the money that is invested in the fleet is obtained from internal business resources or borrowed from outsiders, allocating resources in a particular way deprives one of the interest or return that would be obtained if the monies were invested in a bank or spent in another way.

Once an investment decision has been made the capital is fixed. The choice has been made and the decision has to stand. This is what is usually implied by the term "standing costs." But the decision is not made forever, and there comes a time when a fresh decision must be made. In the long run no costs are standing costs. Nevertheless, it must be remembered that allocation of a fixed cost over short periods of time is quite arbitrary. It may be convenient to depreciate the value of a vehicle equally over the years of its life but it would be equally sensible to recover all the cost in the first year and then have it "for free." There would naturally be dangers in this latter practice. If there were no "cost" allowed in later years, there might be a risk of holding a sum for replacement which will be inadequate when replacement is due. The replacement cost is best measured at frequent intervals and assessed at current prices, the best interval between reassessment being about three months for most transport equipment.

Where a large fleet is involved, of course, vehicles can be taken out of service at intervals. Thus the overall investment in vehicles is almost the same all the time. Where only a few vehicles are employed, however, the opportunity for rethinking one's commitment happens only at the point in time at which a vehicle has to be renewed.

Vehicles may last for their expected life, or they may fail mechanically or become obsolescent. A wise operator allows for some replacement before the end of the attributed technical life. This has the probable consequence of lower maintenance costs, too, as vehicles need more attention in later years than in earlier years.

15

The importance of this longevity of investment is emphasised by the nature of the "product" produced in transport. The product, or service, "perishes the instant of its production." Therefore there is a tendency to estimate costs in terms of the ton carried or the journey performed. This is further encouraged by the selling of transport in terms of tons or journeys. It is natural that one should seek to assess costs in a form suitable to be used as a measure against sales.

Such conventional comparisons can conceal many traps for the unwary. Average costs fail to highlight the wide difference in costs between regular full load operations and operations which only occasionally result in a vehicle being loaded to capacity. They also fail to highlight the character of the return movement which may be loaded instead of empty. It usually fails to show the additional costs which result from delay whilst awaiting loading at a firm's premises. This may cause the vehicle to be back too late to be used for another load.

If the effect on cost of these variations in operation were minor, or the transport industry were less competitive than it is, the problem would not be so great. But the differences in cost which result are considerable and the competitive situation often allows only slender margins. The reaping of marginal advantage in transport can therefore assume an importance which, in a manufacturing business, is not always so evident.

Perhaps this is best illustrated by reference to the railways' problems. Here the operator is faced with investment in vehicles and track which lasts even longer than the investments of the road haulier. He therefore has a high cost which he is committed to for many years. The costs which vary with the amount of traffic put through the system are, over a period of years, often much less than the academic would have us believe. This, of course, is not to say that wagon fleets cannot be reduced nor that staff, a major item in any transporter's cost, cannot be permitted to leave without replacement. Unless the railway operator achieves an optimum throughput of traffic for his high capacity machine, his unit costs are bound to be high. If, by attempting to allocate costs to the ton moved or the journey performed, the variation in costs is overlooked and marginal advantages are not taken into account, then the overall situation is almost bound to deteriorate.

Fortunately the private distributor and the road haulage carrier are blessed in that their track is paid for through a licence charged per vehicle. They therefore avoid the indivisibility of the burden of track costs which the railways face. It may be argued, of course, that the costs of "track," the roads used by the lorries, which it is claimed are imposed on the road carrier through fuel tax and vehicle tax, are excessively onerous, but this is another story. It is one that will be told by politicians and others. The charges must be accepted by the transport manager. He may grumble that, in the national perspective, high taxation on road freight operation inhibits economic development and he may be right.

Most transport operations are subject to the disciplines of budgetary and accountancy control. It is therefore a convention to assess "standing costs" which involve time on an annual basis and then to sub-divide them as necessary. Running costs which vary with mileage are more easily computed for each journey. Wages and overheads should probably be allocated on a time basis.

Whilst these costs will now be discussed in more detail, it should be re-emphasised that allocation of costs to small units of goods distributed is arbitrary even though sometimes useful as a rule of thumb. All too frequently the use of sensible accountancy estimates has caused inefficient management through a lack of understanding. Allocation of the time cost of a vehicle, which may last for seven to ten years, to the movement of a 56 pound (25 kg) package on a conventional basis has often about the same merit as that of allocating all the costs to drivers with red hair and none to those with brown eyes.

Standing costs

Provision for replacement

The purchase price of the vehicle is conventionally divided by the number of years it is estimated that the vehicle will last.

The actual "life" of the vehicle is judged not only on the sturdiness of the vehicle but also by the probable rate of obsolescence. Except in highly specialised product movement, however, obsolescence is less relevant in this age of mass production. Modern equipment is not designed to last as long as it used to be. A large vehicle is normally only expected to last five to eight years, whilst many operators sell vehicles well before this. The number of miles the vehicle is run is pertinent. Vehicles wear not only with time but also with miles travelled.

With the withdrawal of a vehicle from service, the non-committed or running costs of the old equipment should be compared to standing and running costs of the new equipment. However, it will be demonstrated later that provision costs are usually considerably outweighed per vehicle mile or per ton carried by other costs. If a vehicle becomes hard to maintain in serviceable condition, then this will affect its availability, reduced availability will lead to poor utilisation and so on. A good buy is therefore one where the vehicle is off the road for the minimum time.

As capital must be made available to provide equipment, it is a cost of provision to obtain that capital, entailing an interest or a borrowing charge. It is usual for a firm to provide at least some of its transport equipment from its own resources and so it will probably charge against the investment a rate of return which it deems it would have earned from alternatives available to it.

Once the investment is made it may be considered desirable in the accounts to keep the interest charge separate and to show it "below the line" together with profit, shown as part of the firm's earnings. The allowances for interest set aside from time to time, again whether the money is used in the business or not, will earn interest or some other return. These monies are comparable to the interest charge on the capital invested.

The provision calculation is conveniently made by the straight-line method.

The straight-line method. Assume purchase of a £3000 vehicle to be kept in use for six years. The amount to be set aside each year, to allow for replacement, would be £500. Interest at 8 per cent a year on these amounts is shown below:

YEAR	MONIES SET ASIDE AT END OF YEAR	INTEREST EARNED
	£	£
1	500	
2	1000	40
3	1500	80 + 40 = 120
4	2000	120 + 120 = 240
5	2500	160 + 240 = 400
6	3000	200 + 400 = 600

Had money been set aside more frequently than at the end of each year there could have been more than £600 earned. The amount earned would have been about £700.

The actual cost of interest on a £3000 investment for six years at 8 per cent a year is not six years at £240 a year or a total of £1440, but this amount less about £700.

If the rate of interest to be charged is 8 per cent a year, then a convenient way of estimating the cost is to divide the rate by two and calculate at 4 per cent a year. This observation allows the introduction of a simple rule and method of calculation. In order to assess the cost of interest on a renewable asset, the capital invested should be multiplied by half the adopted rate of interest. In the example £720 would have been set aside instead of £740.

Use of the straight-line method of calculating interest charges is simple. To use the other commonly employed techniques, those of the sinking fund or reducing balance, more calculation is needed. Over the whole life of the asset, however, the calculations result in nearly the same answer and for most practical purposes the simple straight-line method is found to be satisfactory.

Insurance

The cost of insuring a vehicle against the normal risks of accident and theft and fire and other perils may be considered merely as a means of sharing the burden of risk among those subscribing to the insurance company through premiums.

Premiums depend on the liability the insurance company is asked to accept and the risk involved, assessed normally on the previous record of claims made. It therefore pays not to make claims for small amounts. As rates are not always the same, it also pays to shop around.

Licences

The Excise (Road Fund) Licence Duty is based on unladen weight of vehicles. In addition, a carrier's licence is necessary. The carrier's licence costs little compared to that of the excise licence. Licences for drivers are also comparatively cheap.

Wages

Minimum wages are controlled for public carriers by the Road Haulage Wages Council which issues Orders stipulating minima. These usually provide a criterion on which more generous payments are based in order that suitable drivers can be secured and retained. To this basic pay must be added National Health Insurance, Superannuation Payments, subsistence allowances when drivers are away from home, bonuses for safe driving and payments under any productivity schemes that may be negotiated. With the continuation of a high level of industrial activity in this country and the need to secure the services of responsible men to drive expensive vehicles without supervision in modern traffic conditions, it is perhaps more suitable to consider wages as the cost of providing a driving staff and thus as a standing rather than a running cost. Temporary diminutions of activity are no longer a justification for dispensing with the services of suitable men, for once lost they can only with difficulty be regained. Good staff may even be recruited to cater for short-term future growth in activity. Statutory obligation to make redundancy payments to men laid off is a minor matter compared to the benefits which result from a good team of drivers.

Once the staff is decided upon, allowances must be made for holidays. For a big fleet, extra staff will be required, whilst for a smaller fleet the problem of covering work to be done can sometimes be solved by using other staff or rearranging the work. Neither of these arrangements is very satisfactory. If it can be arranged, more work may be handed to carriers, but higher than normal charges must be considered in such situations.

Even where high salaries are paid and bonuses are adequate there may be a substantial turnover in staff both in trunking and distribution operation. If it is not possible to hire outside vehicles and men to provide the service required during a shortfall of staff, the cost of having more men during off-peak operations to allow peaks to be accommodated must be taken into account.

Running costs

Fuel

Given the high level of taxation on both diesel oil and petrol, fuel is such a high cost that it is desirable to keep detailed records of each vehicle's consumption of fuel. Consumption per vehicle/mile will give a reasonable guide to cost. The suitability of different grades of fuel in different types of operations can be tested. If large quantities of fuel are required, special terms can often be negotiated with suppliers. If fuel is issued through a privately owned pump the cost of providing and manning the pump may offset the financial advantage of bulk buying. Because fuel consumption obviously varies considerably with the type of operation, it would be unreasonable to compare the fuel used by a small vehicle on a start/stop delivery service with the fuel consumption of a big trunker on a long distance run.

Lubricants

Discounts may also be arranged for the purchase of oil. Expenditure on oil is best included as a running cost but the costs of lubrication may be included with maintenance, especially if a standard maintenance scheme is being operated.

Tyres

The cost of tyres and their replacement will be excluded from standing costs as they are in large part determined by the mileage. Again, the amount of wear depends on the sort of work the vehicle undertakes and it also depends on the terrain, whether traffic is heavy or light and much stopping and starting is necessary and whether the vehicle is driven with care. Wear also depends on whether the pressures are appropriate for the vehicle and its load. There is now a legal obligation not to operate a vehicle with tyres under- or over-inflated. The economics of operating with retreads, especially if a vehicle is involved in motorway high speed movement, should be examined with care.

Maintenance

It is not easy to estimate the cost of maintenance. Good records usually ensure good management and regular preventative maintenance is of growing importance. New legislation is regularising standards, although the cost of ministry inspection is likely to become an extra to be reckoned with and there will be concern about differing interpretations of rules at different testing stations, despite the intent to standardise.

The cost of maintenance may be considered partly as a cost related to time and partly to the distance run. As, for most operators, there is a fairly constant ratio between time and mileage, it seldom matters whether the costs of maintenance are considered as "time" or "mileage."

Vehicle washing

One of the advantages of running one's own vehicles is to keep an "image" of the firm before the public; to keep it a good "image," vehicles should be kept clean and smart. Where a vehicle is driven by only one driver, there is a tendency for the driver to take a pride in his vehicle's appearance, but where

vehicles are on trunking runs and schedules are tight, inter-
change of drivers leads sometimes to a neglect in the vehicle's
appearance. It is true that it is the inside of a van that matters,
yet, nevertheless, vehicle washing equipment is becoming as
necessary as other maintenance facilities.

Loss and damage

Whilst relatively unimportant for bulk movements, the incidence
of loss and damage for smaller consignments of easily marketable
products is sometimes high, having material bearing on the cost
of transport. Although irregular in incidence, it is best taken into
account as a "running" cost, but it may be more appropriately
considered a "standing" cost if insurance cover is taken out for
loss or damage to goods in transit.

Sundry costs

The operation of vehicles involves telephone calls, charges for
parking and garaging and possibly occasional fines. Moreover,
a cost to be considered is that of both the time and the materials
used in the preparation of documents, consignment notes,
delivery schedules, and log sheets.

Overheads

In addition to standing costs, wages, and running costs, there
are the costs of premises, parking areas, goods in transit insurance (if this is substituted for the direct allocation of loss
and damage on particular traffics or movements), supervision,
and general management which must be allocated to transport.
It is arguable that even for a company's own transport a small
profit should be earned. General management costs in particular can only be allocated on an arbitrary basis.

Because of the difficulty in making a generally acceptable
allocation of these costs to individual movements, a practice
normally adopted is to make a 10 or 20 per cent addition to all
other costs as a contribution to overheads. This is an unhappy
convention. It is better to attempt an allocation on a more
satisfactory basis, say on the facilities used and management

Registered number	Date bought	
Vehicle make	Price	
Chassis	Planned life	
description	Estimated residual value	
Body	Taxation weight	

	STANDING COSTS	
	£ a year	Cost a week (year ÷ 47)
Provision for replacement and interest		
Insurance (or loss and damage)		
Licence		

	WAGES	
	£ a month	Cost a week (month ÷ 4)
Wages of driver (gross including NHI, etc)		
Wages of attendant (gross including NHI, etc)		
Bonus		
Subsistence		

	RUNNING COSTS	
	£ a mile	Cost a week (× average weekly mileage)
Fuel		
Lubricant		
Tyres		
Washing allocation		
Sundry costs allocation		
Maintenance		

	OVERHEADS	
	£ a year	Cost a week (year ÷ 47)
Allocation of premises, garage space, and parking space		
Supervision		
General management		
Clerical costs		

FIGURE 2:1 RECORD FOR VEHICLE COST DATA

required in respect of particular operations, or to ignore overheads for particular operations and include them only in total for the whole fleet for the period under consideration. This ought to remind the manager that even though ignored for costing purposes, they are still there and have to be met.

24

	Mileage	Areas	Trips	Drops	Units or Tonnage
Vehicle registered number........ Depot......................			Function: trunking/interfactory movement/delivery		
Monday Tuesday Wednesday Thursday Friday Saturday					
Total					

FIGURE 2:2   RECORD FOR VEHICLE ACTIVITY PER WEEK

Costing documentation

The basic information considered above may be compiled on sheets similar to those exemplified in Figures 2:1–2. This should be assembled with available operating data. It should be supported by dossiers of bills for repairs, maintenance, wages, and so on.

A simple form will often be found useful to make an estimate of the cost of an operation. It can then be kept in a loose-leaf folder for future reference as a standard. This is not part of a formal control system but a formalisation of an estimate of the costs of a particular situation. It is worth noting that a reasonable vehicle utilisation is forty-seven weeks out of the fifty-two in the year although some of the best operators get more and the worst get less than this.

A cost estimate of this kind for one context might be quite unsuitable for another, so an indication of the use to which the estimate is to be put is essential. For example, a vehicle operating from a depot in the Midlands might have a chance back load from the North East. The relevant costs in that situation would be different from those pertinent to the away journey from the Midlands.

To illustrate the way such estimates are of use, some examples

25

are given of different types of vehicle operations in Figures 2:3, 2:4 and 2:5. It will be seen that the cost estimate is in two parts:

1   The cost of providing the equipment and staff to produce the service.
2   Use of the capacity so provided.

		£ WEEK	£ DAY
1	Vehicle standing cost	5	
2	Wages	25	
3	Running costs 200 miles (322 km) a week	4	
		34	6-16 (£6.80)
4	Allocation of overheads	5	1
		£39	£7-16 (£7.80)

Cost a day = £7-16 (£7.80)
Cost a drop at a customer's premises assuming
25 deliveries a day = 6s 3d (£0.31)
Cost of each package delivered assuming 40
packages delivered a day = 3s 10d (£0.19)

FIGURE 2:3   COST ESTIMATE: VEHICLES ON DELIVERY WORK

In this operation packages of about 28 pounds (14.7 kg) weight are delivered to accessible points in urban areas one or two packages at a time. Diesel vans of 15 hundredweight (762 kg) capacity are used.

		£ A WEEK	£ A JOURNEY
1	Vehicle standing cost	20	4
2	Wages	30	6
3	Running cost—200 loaded and 50 empty miles (80.5 km)		13
			23
4	Allocation of overheads	10	2
			25

Cost for each ton carried $= \frac{25}{7} =$ £3-1-6 (£3.07$\frac{1}{2}$) a ton

FIGURE 2:4   COST ESTIMATE: 200 MILE JOURNEY IN 10 TON LORRY

For example, collection of a 7 ton load in London which is to be delivered in Manchester to three customers, 1 ton, 2 tons, and 4 tons respectively. The load is fairly bulky in relation to weight and fills the lorry. A back load has been arranged from Liverpool.

		£ A WEEK	£ A TRIP
1	Vehicle standing cost	30	2
2	Wages	30	2
3	Running cost for 60 miles (96 km) return empty included		4-10 (£4.50)
			8-10 (£8.50)
4	Allocation of overheads	10	-13 (£0.65)
			9-3 (£9.15)

Cost a journey = £9-3-0 (£9.15)

Cost for each ton carried = 12s. 2½d. (£0.61)

FIGURE 2:5   COST ESTIMATE: VEHICLES ON TIPPING WORK
Intensive use of a large lorry capable of carrying 15 tons of a basic raw material from, say, a quarry to a processing plant. The round trip distance is 60 miles (96 km) and provided the vehicles are always available for work each vehicle runs three round trips each working day.

Utilisation of facilities

The second step, that of achieving maximum utilisation of the equipment, is very soon appreciated as important by transport men. It outweighs substantially the value of making economies in providing the capacity. Economies, of course, should not be neglected, but marginal discounts of 5 and 10 per cent in purchasing equipment have a relatively small effect on the unit cost of operation, whereas the achievement of better loads or more deliveries usually has a greater impact. The two simple illustrations in Figures 2:6 and 2:7 show this.

Success in such situations leads to greater efficiency. If we consider private vehicle operation, the efficiency reflects itself in the improved profits of the business, which could mean more capital available for attractive investments in transport. If we are

COST OF EACH JOURNEY	COST/TON WITH A LOAD OF					
	4 TONS	6 TONS	8 TONS	10 TONS	12 TONS	14 TONS
£25	£6-5*	£4-3	£3-2-6	£2-10	£2-1-6	£1-15-9*
	(£6.25)	(£4.15)	(£3.12½)	(£2.50)	(£2.07½)	(£1.79)

FIGURE 2:6   COST OF JOURNEYS WITH LOAD THROUGHOUT

27

	COST PER WEEK				
	£30	£40	£50	£60	£70
PACKAGES DELIVERED		UNIT COST OF DELIVERY			
100	6s (£0.30)	8s (£0.40)	10s (£0.50)	12s (£0.60)	14s* (£0.70)
200	3s (£0.15)	4s (£0.20)	5s (£0.25)	6s (£0.30)	7s (£0.35)
300	2s (£0.10)	2s 8d (£0.13½)	3s 4d (£0.16½)	4s (£0.20)	4s 8d (£0.23½)
400	1s 6d (£0.07½)	2s (£0.10)	2s 6d (£0.12½)	3s (£0.15)	3s 6d (£0.17½)
500	1s 3d* (£0.06)	1s 8d (£0.08½)	2s (£0.10)	2s 5d (£0.12)	2s 10d (£0.14)

FIGURE 2:7   UNIT COST OF DELIVERY

considering carriers, low costs allow charges to be lowered. As soon as charges are below those of competitive services, assuming acceptability of the service to the customer, demand for the service tends to increase. This increased demand leads to more intensive utilisation of equipment and to yet further lowering of costs.

Not only is better use of the equipment associated with a satisfactory throughput, but the men working the equipment to provide a service tend to react favourably to what is obviously an efficient operation. Even if the economic improvements are not directly reflected in terms of bonus, the pride that most transport men have in their jobs (but often attempt to conceal) encourages maximum effort to maintain efficiency.

The actual process of assessing the costs of an operation is usually at least as valuable and instructive as the answer itself. Areas of high cost are highlighted and the significance of particular practices becomes obvious.

When undertaking such exercises it is important that a sufficiently long period of time is taken into consideration in order to avoid distortion of the situation as the result of short-term fluctuations of traffic.

What emerges from such investigations is that the advantages of specialisation are only maximised when the specialised equipment is fully employed. There is little use, for example, in having enough vehicles to cope with peak traffic if in extensive off-peak periods the vehicles are underemployed. Equally, vehicles designed for motorways are of little use if much of their running time is spent away from motorways. Use of averages is obviously dangerous when the number of operations is small and varied such as is often the case for a small fleet. Inappropriate averages can falsify the conclusion drawn. Unless adequate allowances are made in the overall assessment for such possibilities there is a risk of undercosting the operation of small fleets. Vehicles especially designed to carry palletised loads are uneconomic if they have to be used to carry commodities which are not suitable for palletisation or if a poorer vehicle pay load, resulting from the use of pallets, plus the cost of the pallets outweigh the reduced cost of handling.

The estimates become "snapshots" of economic situations. The estimates are designed to illustrate particular situations in a particular sector of the business and to give a basis on which managerial action may be taken. The accounts provide "film" for record purposes. The figures produced for the accounts can and should be used as an effective control on the sum of the snap-shots produced. The accountancy figures can be designed to provide the material for the snapshots. This interdependence between the cost estimate and the accountancy system should be encouraged. In a sense, the accountant proves success or failure whilst the manager, with his estimated figures, produces pointers which may lead to improved results.

Summary of chapter

1   Cost may be understood as not having one thing in order to have something else.

2   For convenience the cost of making the choice is measured in monetary terms.

3   If the company is to remain in business then not only must there be expenditure to maintain and operate equipment but there must also be a provision for replacement and an allowance for the capital investment.

4   Conventions in allocation of cost over the life of equipment or in estimations of cost by the ton or for each journey conceal traps for the unwary.

5   As competition in transport often only allows slender profit margins it is important to understand which costs are relevant in particular situations.

6   Costs of vehicles may be divided into:

(a) Standing costs
including provision for replacement
insurance
licences.

(b) Wages.

(c) Running costs
including fuel
lubricants
tyres
maintenance
vehicle washing
loss and damage
sundry costs.

(d) Overheads.

7   A cost estimate in one situation may be quite unsuitable for use in another.

8   It will be seen from estimates that the assessment of cost is in two parts:

(a) The cost of providing the equipment and staff to produce the service.

(b) Use of the capacity so provided.

9   Achieving maximum utilisation of the capacity provided substantially outweighs the value of making economies in providing capacity, though these should not be neglected.

10   The process of cost assessment is valuable in that it highlights the areas of high cost.

11   Estimates should be like snapshots of particular situations. They should be controlled by production of accounts and the two activities should be interdependent.

THREE

Basic approach to fleet planning

The argument that the introduction of scientific techniques will solve business problems is less convincing in transport than it might be in other businesses. Transport men are usually by training independent and practical and there are so many variations of the basic problems.

Perhaps the best combination would be to practise the sophisticated scientific methodology with an understanding of the details of a firm's transport operations. Unfortunately, this understanding is seldom gained except by much practical experience and it is rare to find such experience in combination with a predilection for the mathematical techniques required in operational analysis, linear programming, critical path analysis or the programming of computers. Without practical know-how resulting from experience, there is a temptation to simplify the input to a computer or over-simplify the basis on which an econometric model is built. The results of the exercise can then be demonstrably inappropriate for one set of circumstances, thus reducing the credibility of the results produced for other sets of circumstances.

For many decades transport has been regarded merely as a burden of cost to the manufacturer. This attitude has tended to persist even with the growth of private fleets. Use of private fleets has been very much regarded as a way in which to provide a service which should be reasonably efficient but would inevitably involve a high cost.

But the introduction of the discipline of scientific methods does lead to better results. Where these methods are applied intelligently and not mechanically and where they are adjusted in the light of experience gained during use, advantage can be taken of the transport experience and understanding of the operators. This is in contrast with situations where problems are to be solved automatically, possibly using a computer, and where there is no chance to evaluate the evidence as it is fed in or to learn as the exercise progresses. When using a computer everything must be planned in detail before the start, which is seldom easy. Often, of course, it is not a scientific method that pays off but merely the widespread application of formalised common sense.

Size of fleet

The split of traffic between one's own vehicles and use of carriers is discussed in greater detail in Chapter 5. How much is transported in own vehicles and therefore how many vehicles are needed is subject to adjustments as costs of transport and carriers' charges change. Not infrequently, and often wrongly, as many own vehicles appear to be employed as seem to be the maximum likely to be needed for the traffic. To decide how many vehicles are the optimum number, it is preferable to examine traffic it is required to move over a period.

It is necessary to choose an appropriate period. The nature of the transport services to be provided must be borne in mind. The period should be long enough to avoid the effect of occasional or seasonal variations. It should be short enough to be manageable in the analysis.

The figures must then be modified in accordance with probable developments in production trends. For those who are so inclined, the arithmetic mean, standard deviation, a table of probabilities, and of probability of accuracy may be calculated. What might to most people be undesirable mathematical calculations may, however, be avoided by plotting the daily vehicle requirements and anticipated future requirements on a graph for the representative period.

This easier method has two advantages, the first of which is the imprecision of the graphical method emphasises the imprecision of the assumptions which of necessity are made when guessing the number of vehicles required. If it is a delivery operation being considered, the number of deliveries a day can vary and such variations are almost impossible to define with precision at peak times and off-peak times. Traffic conditions will change and trunk operators may or may not achieve the standard they set for operations.

The second advantage is that the graphical demonstration of requirements is often an asset when clarifying the nature of an argument. It is useful when attempting to persuade one's

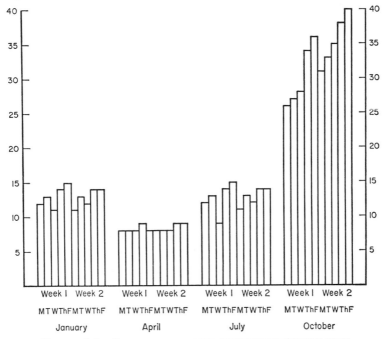

FIGURE 3:1   SEASONAL ANALYSIS OF VEHICLE REQUIREMENTS
The vertical scale shows vehicles required.

superiors. It is perhaps most useful when demonstrating the problem and its possible solution to members of a board not always notorious for their acumen. The possible situation might be as is shown in Figure 3:1.

It is not often that a firm has to plan its transport fleet without some previous experience. Usually there is already a fleet in existence. When this is the case, intelligent scrutiny of requirements in detail should lead to a staged reduction or staged increase in the fleet in order that at each stage a check may be made of the results. In this way there is a chance to verify the correctness of the action.

Let there be no illusions. If an overlarge fleet of vehicles is provided it will be used. An overlarge fleet will make life easier for many people. It will not maximise profit.

Daily requirements

Clearly marginal vehicles are required less frequently than the so-called hard core. This does not mean that vehicles will necessarily stand about. Supply the vehicles and jobs of one kind or another will be found for them. The work to be done will spread over all the vehicles available, with the result that the general level of vehicle utilisation is lowered. In the example, between eleven and fifteen vehicles are required for use every day of the working week, ten vehicles are required on most occasions. An attempt should be made at this stage to allocate the whole year's standing cost to the marginal vehicles and to determine the cost per vehicle on this basis. Such an exercise is illustrated in Figure 3:2.

Similarly, vehicles which are scheduled for regular maintenance will be unavailable for operations. One must accept, too, that vehicles are inclined to break down and will therefore be unavailable even allowing for a regular schedule of maintenance. Not only are vehicles inclined to failure, but drivers, too, have the normal drawbacks of oversleeping, changing jobs, and sickness and their absences can cause an otherwise available vehicle to be unoperational.

APPROXIMATE NUMBER OF DAYS REQUIRED FOR USE		VEHICLES IN FLEET SHOWING MARGINAL ADDITIONS	APPROXIMATE STANDING COST A DAY FOR EACH VEHICLE ADDED
10	At high peak	5	£75
20	At high peak	5	£32-10 (£32.50)
25	At high peak	5	£30
30	Only during autumn peak	10	£25
200	Most days except in spring off peak	5	£3-15 (£3.75)
250	Most days	10	£3

FIGURE 3:2   COSTING OF MARGINAL VEHICLES

A reasonable margin for nonavailability could vary from 5 to 25 per cent. The smaller margin might apply in the case of a highly organised and disciplined large fleet. If a small fleet is being operated over long distances on a widely geographical pattern the number of vehicles required as spares could be very high.

The cost of keeping vehicles to cater for the peak could be very much higher than the costs of hiring, if hiring is possible during the peak. If hiring is impossible, however, due to the nature of the service which demands provision of specialised vehicles or if it is impossible for the goods to be held back because of their perishable nature, at least those that demand the service should be aware of the high cost of providing the marginal vehicles. It may be that only in this way will those responsible for requiring a particular service be made aware of the costs involved and therefore of the possible advantages of changing their requirements. If, for example, the service demanded can be altered with only modest expenditure on the production side or modest loss of sales, it could be to the overall advantage of the firm to change the transport pattern.

Distribution problems

The number of deliveries possible is determined by the distance between customers or drops of goods, the nature of the terrain, the density of the traffic, and the ease with which delivery can be effected. Whether or not signatures should be obtained when the deliveries are small is open to debate. Where experiments have been conducted and the collection of signatures has been discontinued the difference in claims has often been remarkably small. The time taken for a driver to ensure he has got the appropriate signature on his load sheet often outweighs a marginal benefit.

The problems of delivery at firms' premises or on construction sites are various. Unloading delays, however, are rarely eliminated by the imposition of customer penalties or incentives. Penalties are commercially difficult to impose. Incentives can rarely be made sufficiently attractive to induce a customer to change what may be a long established habit of work or a practice which is of value to him. Often the most satisfactory solution is achieved by the encouragement of a sound working relationship with the customer, either directly manager to manager or by means of the contacts made by the driver or both. Suggestions to promote co-operation in delivery to mutual advantage can at least be discussed.

In urban areas there are experiments, some of which have proved successful, to open a firm's premises in the evening hours after the normal work has finished. Thus delivery vehicles can move and stand in streets which have become comparatively empty and avoid delays imposed by traffic congestion and by recipients of goods being engaged elsewhere.

The outstanding example of delay in reception is where goods are tendered to warehouses in dock areas or at a ship's side. Delays here have been known to have amounted to more than two days on occasions and the queues of vehicles awaiting reception and discharge at most of our major docks are notorious. The dock authorities complain that manufacturers dispatch only in time for delivery to be made on the last days that vessels are "open" for receiving cargo. Manufacturers reply that the difficulties of their own business make easier delivery schedules impossible. A possible solution to reception at the docks may be in the extension of the "appointment" arrangements so that lorries can book themselves in for unloading and can be reasonably sure of a departure in time for pre-planned subsequent operation.

Undoubtedly efficiency in delivery is enhanced by the introduction of suitable bonus systems. Bonus systems are best designed to have a marked incentive to a particular level of efficiency and marked disincentive thereafter. If this level of efficiency is acceptable to both men and managers this avoids the possible maltreatment of packages in the attempt to maximise bonus at the risk of damage or even loss.

Routeing

Only rarely is there the chance of planning routes on a regular basis. There is, however, a good case for the betterment of general practices as a result of past experience. This can be done by preparing a "string" diagram of previous operations so that excessive mileages and uneconomic diversions may be highlighted and avoided in future operations. The best job is probably done by those who have had personal experience in driving heavy lorries. They are aware of the problems of operating in certain areas and along certain routes, are aware of drivers' preferences and dislikes, times of traffic congestion, conditions in both winter and summer and the mass of detail which distinguishes between possibilities and impossibilities.

It is known, for example, for the business of a firm to require a changed distribution pattern but for drivers who have to spend a night away from home to persist in using familiar overnight stopping places. Equally, when a driver is asked at the last moment to include urgent orders in a round which he has determined for himself, it may be difficult for him to avoid going first to the customer with the urgent order either to satisfy the urgency of the demand or merely to clear a space on his vehicle so that the other deliveries may be made in the logical manner in which the load was built up.

After the order has been assembled for a vehicle operation and an indication of optimum routeing made, it is usually best to leave the actual operation to the driver, especially if he earns a bonus from efficient operation. Even in noncapitalist societies men quickly find the easiest way to complete their work. When there is also a financial incentive, it is remarkable how efficiently and easily success can be achieved.

Routeing where expensive and specialised equipment is involved needs to be more than ever highly disciplined so that utilisation can be intensive. Where desirable, changeover of drivers can be arranged at points on the route but for this to be reliable there must be built into the schedule a flexibility of operation. With this flexibility the advantages of specialisation are decreased. It is not true that all drivers like to get home at night. Where they do or when their wives bring pressure to bear, the additional costs of a changeover of drivers, the time involved and the extra time to give the flexibility of operation that is required must be offset against the extra costs of overnight subsistence payment to cover food and lodging.

Given the location of drops and the character of the load, the useful work possible with each vehicle, average speeds for town and country driving and such other restrictions and good use of equipment and men, who have already been mentioned, it is possible to use computers to work out optimum loads and schedules. It is usually far too onerous to attempt the whole of such a job by hand. But with the large number of variations required on input the distribution model constructed often turns out to be unreal. Some big firms who have used programmes of distribution produced by a computer are known to have abandoned them. There are examples of many months' computer work being completed only for the result to show 16 ton vehicles regularly travelling over a bridge which was known to have a 5 ton limit. Another major exercise was completely nullified because, in a comparison between road and rail, a 2 ton rate was assumed by the programmers to mean up to 2 ton, whereas in fact it meant 2 to 4 ton. Perhaps the best compromise is a detailed analysis by hand in selected representative areas and the application of the principles established over the whole distribution area to be covered. Even those who start out by aiming to control their distribution scheduling by computer often change their minds in the course of their feasibility studies.

Measurement of standard cost factors

In whatever way the trunking or distribution analysis is elaborated, there are two factors to be measured. The first is *time* and the second is *distance*. These factors must be measured in terms of the units carried. There are different ways of doing this.

Vehicle day and mileage analysis

By inspection, operations are grouped into those possible each vehicle day and the mileage is assessed. The vehicle day is then measured by a factor to include the vehicle costs which accrue on a time basis plus the costs of the driver and other vehicle staff. The costs of running this type of vehicle are then applied to the mileage. Each vehicle's probable load is determined and a cost per ton carried worked out.

Use of standard times

Various relevant operations are measured using work study techniques and reduced to per ton and per mile standards. Totals of the proposed operations are then made and multiplied per ton and mile by the standards.

Computers are more easily adapted to processing the data assembled for the second method. The first method on the other hand allows the analyst to make adjustments to the pattern of operation and to isolate areas for improvement. Standards used in the second method tend to get out of date and are much too frequently used blindly. The second method therefore tends to be used for bigger fleet operations.

Motorways and specialist vehicles

To take most advantage of using the growing network of motorways, vehicles must be capable of high speeds, rapid acceleration for overtaking, and reliability. Rapid acceleration is important because freight vehicles are only allowed to use two lanes where the motorway is three-lane. For safe operation they should be able to overtake quickly even when fully loaded. If a vehicle has insufficient acceleration to allow it to pass, then to be held back behind a slow-moving vehicle may waste considerable time advantage. Bunching of vehicles on a motorway is potentially dangerous, especially if the bunch is travelling at a high speed. Thus to use motorways to best advantage vehicles are designed for power and speed. This does not necessarily conform to requirements away from the motorways. There, smaller and lighter vehicles may be needed with better performance at lower speeds.

It is in part because of this growing need for specialisation in vehicles that the case for articulation and containerisation is growing. In both instances the tractors or power units can be intensively employed whilst the container, articulated body or skeletal chassis can be detached for loading and unloading or even for temporary storage.

In the case of articulated vehicles the problem of jack-knifing cannot be with us much longer. It is true at the moment that certain counties' police forces will forbid the operation of articulated vehicles along roads which are dangerous in winter. This can ruin a highly organised, intensive, low-cost trunk operation. But already devices which seem to be effective are being introduced to avoid these disadvantages and they are likely to become much more effective as experience grows.

Integration with rail services

British Rail's salesmen's claims for the future role of the railways vary. There even seems to be conflict among the railway managers as to the part to be played in the future by the railway system. One thing is clear. British Rail has a potential winning service with (a) company trains and (b) Freightliner services.

Excellent concepts though these are, and neither is new except in its presentation and in its livery, they are unlikely to become the widespread trunk haulage system that they are sometimes hailed to be by over-enthusiastic railway supporters.

Both services provide transport which at last matches that afforded as a matter of course by the public road carrier and is expected of any operation with own vehicles. At most destinations deliveries are made next morning. Between places well over 300 miles apart, such as between London and Scotland and London and the North-East, the rail service is generally faster than the service secured by sending the goods by road.

To be worthwhile, consignments in trainload quantities must be at least about 300 tons. They are therefore restricted to raw materials, semi-finished products and a few consumer goods forwarded by a small number of large firms. These conditions are satisfied in the extractive and basic industries. Once coal, oil, semi-finished steel, pulped paper, iron ore, and motor vehicles are eliminated, there is not much else which can pass regularly in these quantities.

The trainload operation is best from a private siding to a private siding. It has important disadvantages to the railways if it is at all irregular. On the other hand, if in addition to being sent regularly in large consignments the traffic is carried in non-railway-owned wagons and the contract is signed for a long term and includes an "escalation" clause which allows the charge to be varied to take account of changes in the value of money or the railway's costs, then the movement is of the sort that railwaymen like. Charges for such movements are therefore low. If the rail movement is organised efficiently the direct costs can be very low indeed.

It is a sad legacy of once proud and independent systems that more operational difficulties are encountered if the termini of trainload operations happen to be in different management regions. Despite much recent effort to correct this fault, the railwayman is still a conservative at heart. Some managers appear still unaware of the splendid services offered by the best of their competitors. Second-rate unreliable services are un-saleable to manufacturers, whose own efficiency is impaired when this leads to a default in supply or in distribution. It is known that some large firms with a sizeable rail carriage com-mitment employ men to assist BR staff in the determination of priorities and ensuring better service through adequate liaison.

The Freightliner service is a development of the general goods container systems popularised in this country in the 1920s. For decades there has been obvious need for containers larger than the original *B, BD*, and similar types, which produced relatively high unit costs for the 5 tons payload and about 720 cubic feet (20.4 m^3) of space, and the *A*-type container which allowed 3–4 tons and about 320 cubic feet (9.1 m^3). These containers were loaded one to a flat four-wheeled wagon and were lifted on and off the wagon at stations equipped with a crane of suitable capacity. Access to such cranes by rail or road was not always easy and in consequence unit costs of movement were perhaps further raised.

By building new terminals, especially designed to deal with bigger traffic throughputs; by building new wagons and linking them into permanently coupled trains; by building new box and open containers of 30 feet (9.14 m), 20 feet (6.09 m), and 10 feet (3.04 m) in length with weight capacities of 20, 15, and 7½ tons and capacities of 1580, 1050, and 500 cubic feet (44.7 m^3, 29.7 m^3, and 14.2 m^3), the way has been opened for substan-tially better utilisation of both rolling stock and fixed equipment. It is not without some interest perhaps to remember that better use could also have been obtained and can be obtained by the more intensive use of conventional rail equipment. When this is used as intensively as road vehicles are used, the cost reductions a ton carried are very marked. The Freightliner trains are normally of fifteen bogied wagons, each carrying two 20-foot (6.09 m) containers or their equivalent. Special lifting equipment is provided for the terminal road/rail transfer.

The importance of ensuring that this high capacity and

expensive trunking system is well patronised has led to charges being offered per container which are attractive to those for whom the service proves suitable. The railways will bring and collect a container from a firm's premises and will deliver to the customer at destination. This road movement can also be undertaken by one's own vehicle or that of another carrier. Charges may be quoted separately for the terminal to terminal service and for the collection and delivery service.

If the Freightliner is a success, the roles of British Rail and road transport in future years will be reversed. For general goods British Rail has been the residual carrier. Goods in excess of the regular capacity of a firm's own lorries and those of its regular road carriers have been put on rail. This is most marked at times of peak industrial activity or distributive activity. If, as a result of providing low-cost and satisfactory transport, the railways become the service of first choice, the high cost of providing a "standby" service will be passed to road carriers or private fleets. This may also result from Government direction. The owners of these road fleets may or may not choose to accept such a role. If they do not, the resulting deterioration in services will be reflected in higher selling costs for manufactured goods.

Most of the main industrial conurbations in England and Wales are within a couple of hundred miles of each other. The Freightliner services between London and Scotland and London and the North-East are therefore exceptional. A more typical situation is that between London and Manchester, which are about 180 miles (288 km) apart.

The charge for a 20-foot (6.09 m) box or covered container used once from the London terminal to the Manchester terminal is £13. Lower charges are made for round trip working and for regular forwardings or for a large number of containers. To this must be added the charge for the road service to and from the terminal. Within a ten mile radius of the terminal this would add £14 to the charge. For extremely good loading traffic this results in a charge per ton of 36 shillings (£1.80).

Making conventional allocations of cost and allowing a

43

modest profit margin, as undoubtedly must have been the case when the Freightliner charges were determined, road costs amount to about £2 to £2-5 (£2.25) a ton. This therefore gives a competitive advantage to the railways which they can exploit intelligently and which they have not always exploited intelligently in the past. It is not an overwhelming advantage and cannot be treated as such.

The benefits in using the Freightliner are markedly reduced in any of the following circumstances.

1   When the premises from which the goods are forwarded are north of London and the consignee's premises are in a place well south of Manchester, as this means travelling substantial distances to the rail terminal in the wrong direction.

2   When the premises at both ends of the movement are near to a linking motorway, as normally this will reduce a heavy vehicle's costs per journey.

3   If the goods to be conveyed are bulky in relation to their weight, as loads can be built higher on a road vehicle which is not subject to the disciplines of the railway's loading gauge. To get 15 tons into a 20-foot covered container needs a loadability of 70 cubic feet (1.98 m³) a ton, which is considerably lower than most general goods traffic.

4   If the goods are best loaded into the road vehicle from overhead or from the sides of the vehicles or if the depots are equipped for this type of loading. As yet, most of the covered containers are inaccessible from above and most only have end doors.

5   Wherever the times which the containers must be tendered at the railway depot are inconvenient for traffic loading. Railway "acceptance" times are still earlier than would appear commercially convenient.

6   If goods for the Freightliner destination have to be separated from those which otherwise would

be taken as part of a load and dropped on the way. This part of the load must then be sent by separate vehicle or held back.

7   Whenever Freightliner containers remain in short supply and advance booking is required. Advance booking may be incompatible with the delivery pattern of the firm.

8   If the vehicle which is displaced by the Freightliner service is still needed to serve destinations not served by the Freightliner.

9   If the railway staff continue to take strike action to defend their interests in a contracting enterprise and thus stop services or cause delays.

An advantage of the company train and Freightliner service is that there is reduced risk of pilferage unless, in the case of the company train, the wagons are slowed or stopped in a lonely but accessible spot.

The company train and the Freightliner services must be considered when planning supply transport or distribution systems. Both have cost advantages if the traffic to be conveyed is appropriate. There may be other advantages (such as that of reduction of pilferage) which weigh against the system's disadvantages to the user. Should the charge be revised to the point where the cost advantages are insufficient to outweigh the net disadvantages, not only the railways and the potential customers but (as long as the railways remain subject to open or concealed subsidy) also the nation will suffer.

Summary of chapter

1   Solution of transport problems can be aided by the introduction of scientific method.
      The best results are usually obtained by transport men using new techniques intelligently and with care.

2   The size of the fleet is subject to adjustment as costs of transport and carrier's costs change.

3   The number of vehicles is determined by review of the goods to be moved over a representative period. This may be tabulated or shown graphically.

4   Allowance must be made for non-availability of vehicles for useful work because they:

  (*a*) Are in the wrong place.

  (*b*) Are scheduled for maintenance.

  (*c*) Have failed mechanically or a driver is unobtainable.

5   The cost of private vehicles retained to provide for the peak makes the marginal tonnages to be carried extremely expensive. This is so despite concentration of maintenance work into the off peak period.

6   The appropriateness of size of an existing fleet may be tested by marginal adjustment of the number of vehicles.

7   The capacity per vehicle per unit of time involves consideration of the character of the transport to be provided. Distribution and trunking vehicles' utilisation are both affected in part by delays in the tendering of the traffic to the consignee.

8   Good routeing of vehicles increases capacity and reduces mileage cost for each ton moved.

9   Quantification of units of transport as produced by analysis should then be by time and distance. There are two methods:

  (*a*) A vehicle day and mileage analysis.

  (*b*) Use of standard measures.

10   The latter method, if appropriate standards are used has more precision and should therefore be used for analysis of the operation of big fleets. The former allows for greater judgement and is therefore useful for the analysis of smaller fleets.

11   There is not yet much evidence of successful routeing and load planning by computer because of the complexity of the input.

12   Use of motorways encourages greater speed and specialisation.

13   There are benefits to be gained by integrating trunk

operations with British Rail company trains or Freight-liners. Neither of these concepts are new in principle nor do the services surpass those provided by road hauliers except on the routes London to the North-East and to Scotland.

14   The rail services do provide cheap movement for goods which are not bulky in relation to weight.

15   There are a number of disadvantages of using rail and not least among these is the reduction in flexibility of operation which is characteristic of road operation.

16   Should the net cost advantage outweigh the disadvantages of using the service, and this in large part will be determined by the pricing policy of the Freightliner company, then the shape of national product distribution could well be changed.

FOUR

Realities of capital investment in transport

The firm's corporate strategy for the investment of its resources will rarely be the immediate concern of the transport manager, except in so far as this strategy concerns transport or distribution operations. Some investments are essential to the welfare of the firm's operation, such as access roads, parking areas, and properly equipped loading bays. These are provided when factory production is decided upon and without them there would be no production at all.

A firm can choose, however, between having the simplest of equipment and having more expensive equipment. Anything more than the minimum should be the subject of an investment appraisal.

Investment in plant or vehicles for the transportation of goods can only be at the expense of investment in the business elsewhere or investment outside the firm. In the long run a soft answer from a sweet-voiced secretary is not nearly so effective as the availability of another truck. The transport manager must therefore be prepared to co-operate with the financial department in the preparation of schemes for transport which will be weighed against other schemes which fall within the firm's corporate planning.

Traditional methods

The method of assessing the return on an investment which used to be employed was to measure the increase in the net return and compare this to the capital invested.

For example, if four vehicles were bought, each costing £2500, and, making an allowance for maintenance, each vehicle reduced costs so that net revenue increased by £250 a year this would be expressed as:

$$\frac{£1000}{£10\,000} \times 100 = 10\%$$

The return on the investment was 10 per cent. But if we allow for renewal in equal instalments over the life of the vehicles, as was considered in Chapter 2, the actual amount invested in the vehicles would decrease over the years. Assume that the vehicles have a five-year life. Using the "straight-line" method, at the end of the first year the capital invested in the fleet is only £8000, £2000 having been set aside and available for investment elsewhere in the business or earning interest in the bank. At the end of the second year the amount invested would only be £6000. In the third, fourth, and fifth years the amounts will be £4000, £2000, and nil. The average amount invested will be about £5000. Looking at it in this way:

The return on the investment is $\dfrac{£1000}{£5000} \times 100 = 20$ per cent.

Both these calculations fail to take into account taxation. For the sake of this example, let us assume that the level of tax on the firm's earnings is 40 per cent. Tax, of course, will vary with allowances and the availability of grants. At 40 per cent, however, the annual net revenue effect of £1000 will be reduced to £600. Taking into account tax, therefore, the return on the investment in the four vehicles is 6 per cent on the original capital invested and 12 per cent on the average capital invested.

There are two aspects of the investment problem which these techniques do not take into consideration:

1   The effect of investment on net revenue will not be the same year by year. It is probable that there will be more effect in the earlier years and less later on.

2   Investment in those vehicles which are expected to last for five years will need to be compared to investment in other equipment with a shorter or a longer life.

Slightly more sophisticated techniques thus become necessary.

Pay-back method

This is a somewhat colourful technique and without doubt useful when orally presenting a case to a disbelieving board of directors. It is used to establish the number of years required to recoup the initial expenditure. The "pay-back" is the total of the annual improvements in net revenue. Assume that the four vehicles each have a scrap value at the end of their lives of £500. This gives a net investment of £8000. Assume annual net revenue improvements of £2000.

YEAR	IMPROVEMENT IN NET REVENUE	ACCUMULATED TOTAL
	£	£
1	2000	2000
2	2000	4000
3	2000	6000
4	2000	8000

It will take four years to pay back the investment. The fifth year is therefore all profit. But how much is the profit worth in five years' time? This consideration moves us into contemplation of the cash flow.

Discounted cash flow

Obviously the timing of the flow of cash back from an investment is important. The earlier the returns on an investment are realised, the better. If the improvement in net revenue is more in the later stages, this is less satisfactory than if it is realised

50

earlier. The earlier the improvements, the earlier the extra cash can be put to work in other projects.

It is worth reconsidering what happens when an investment is decided upon:

1   A choice is made between alternatives and money is locked up. Once the decision has been made, it must normally stand for the life of the equipment.

2   The earnings from this investment are gradually realised as improvements in net revenue.

3   The residual value of the equipment is realised when the equipment is sold at the end of its life.

Investment involves a decision to deny present consumption in the hope of future gain. Apart from the risk involved in any investment, cash now is worth more than the assurance of cash in the future. To take this into account, future net improvement or cash flows may be "discounted." The value of future gain is related to a gain now. This depends on what could be gained if the investment were not made. As gains get more and more remote from the time the investment is made, so does their present value appear less.

If we buy our four vehicles we invest £10 000. If we leave this money in the bank where the rate of interest is 5 per cent, or in the business where it carries a return of 5 per cent, then at the end of the year the amount owing to us would be £10 500. If this money is not withdrawn, at the end of the second year the amount would be £10 500 plus 5 per cent of £10 500, that is a total of £11 025. This is normal compound interest. It may also be looked at the other way round. The £10 500 in a year's time at a 5 per cent rate of interest is only worth £10 000 now, and £11 025 in two years' time is also worth £10 000 now.

Calculations of this kind can be reduced to formulas or they can be avoided altogether by the use of different tables. (See Figure 4:1.)

To ascertain the present value of £10 000 received in five years' time at 5 per cent, turn to the tables. Under the heading

YEAR	5%	10%	15%
1	0.952	0.909	0.870
2	0.907	0.826	0.756
3	0.864	0.751	0.658
4	0.823	0.683	0.572
5	0.784	0.621	0.497
6	0.746	0.564	0.432
7	0.711	0.513	0.376
8	0.677	0.467	0.327
9	0.645	0.424	0.284
10	0.614	0.386	0.247
11	0.585	0.350	0.215
12	0.557	0.319	0.187
13	0.530	0.290	0.163
14	0.505	0.263	0.141
15	0.481	0.239	0.123
20	0.377	0.149	0.061
25	0.295	0.092	

FIGURE 4:1   DISCOUNT TABLE

5%, trace the column of figures until level with the year 5. The discount factor is 0.784. Multiply this by £10 000 and the answer is:

At 5 per cent of discount to receive £10 000 in five years' time would give a current value of £7840.

Discounted cash flow in practice

To use the DCF method of investment appraisal it is necessary to find a discount rate at which the *present* values of *future* cash benefits are equal to the monies currently invested. The higher the discount rate, the lower will be the present values of the future benefits. The lower the discount rate, the higher will be the values of the future benefits.

An assessment of the present value of benefits for our four vehicles could be as shown at the top of page 53.

At present values, therefore, the return on this investment is a little over 5 per cent. The rate of return is assessed by trial and error and, when the problem is a complicated one, this is

YEAR	IMPROVEMENT IN NET REVENUE	FACTOR FROM DISCOUNT TABLE AT 5%	PRESENT VALUE OF BENEFITS
	£		£
1	2000	0.952	1904
2	2000	0.907	1814
3	2000	0.864	1728
4	2000	0.823	1646
5	2000	0.784	1568
			£8660

Investment (less scrap value): £8000

difficult. For practical purposes, however, an approximate rate of return is normally quite good enough.

If a minimum acceptable rate of return is stipulated for an investment and this is used as the present value factor, then provided the sum of the present values of the benefits year by year exceeds the investment over the life of the equipment, then the investment would be acceptable. If the present values of the future benefits fall short of the money to be invested, then the investment would not be acceptable.

Assume that a firm has alternatives open to it of a kind that leads to the stipulation that a minimum return of 10 per cent is necessary before an investment is made. The investment of £10 000 in new vehicles with the net revenue benefits assumed in our previous examples would not be acceptable and the business should be put out to carriers. If, on the other hand, raised carriers' charges or an increased incidence of damage, leading to extra packaging requirements, happened to coincide with improved fleet operational efficiency, then the prospect of increased future benefits would indicate a reappraisal of the situation. For example, in the following conditions the investment would be acceptable with a postulated return at 10 per cent, even without an allowance for scrap or residual value.

Benefits are not easy to assess. They get less easy to assess as they get further into the future. Beware of both over-optimism or undue pessimism.

Should there be a number of possible investments the returns

YEAR	IMPROVEMENT IN NET REVENUE	FACTORS FROM DISCOUNT TABLE AT 10%	PRESENT VALUE OF BENEFITS
	£		£
1	3000	0.909	2 727
2	3000	0.826	2 478
3	3000	0.751	2 253
4	2000	0.683	1 366
5	2000	0.621	1 242
			£10 066

Investment £10 000, residual value nil

may be conveniently compared by using an index. This can be arrived at by dividing the present value of the benefits at the prescribed discount rate by the investment. Thus in our last example, the index number is:

$$\frac{\text{Present value of benefits}}{\text{Amount invested}} \text{ or } \frac{10\ 066}{10\ 000} \text{ or } 1.0066$$

Other investments may produce an index number of more or less than this.

Implications of taxation

The effect of taxation on investment is substantial. There must be considered:

1   Receipt of any investment grant.
2   Possible allowances reducing the amount of tax to be paid.
3   The time relationship between the payment of taxes and the realisation of the benefits.

Investment grants are cash offers by the Government for certain types of new equipment or plant. These grants only apply to certain industries, and they are higher in the development areas than in other areas of the country. Claims must be made for grants to the Board of Trade. Tax allowances are of three kinds:

1   *Initial allowances.* These are expressed as a percentage of the cost of the equipment less any investment grant.

2   *Writing down allowances.* These are permitted each
year for the life of the equipment. This may be as a
percentage of the written down value of the equipment or a percentage of the original cost less any
investment grant.

3   *Balancing allowances.* When equipment is sold at
the end of its life, the sum realised at the sale is
deducted from the written down value. If the result
is positive, a balancing allowance is credited to
adjust the written allowances to the actual loss
suffered. If the result is negative, the difference
between the allowances made and what should
have been made is adjusted by a balancing charge.

Tax allowances reduce the taxable benefits for the year. If there
are no profits made by the firm against which the allowances
can be made, the allowances may be carried forward.

At present private cars for business get neither investment
grants nor initial allowances. Other vehicles get initial allowances of 30 per cent. Handling equipment and other equipment
in non-development areas, if "qualifying" for an investment
grant, secure one of 20 per cent. If "non-qualifying" there is no
investment grant but an initial allowance of 30 per cent. In
development areas "qualifying" equipment gets a 40 per cent
investment grant and "non-qualifying" gets 30 per cent initial
allowance. New industrial buildings get a 15 per cent initial
allowance in non-development areas and new industrial buildings in development areas get an investment grant of between 25
and 35 per cent and an initial allowance of 15 per cent. Non-
industrial buildings in a non-development area get an investment grant of 25 to 30 per cent only. New ships have the benefit
of a 20 per cent investment grant and thereafter free depreciation.
This means that the firm can claim depreciation at whatever
rates suit the firm rather than at rates prescribed by the tax

people. Secondhand ships get no investment grant but an initial allowance of 30 per cent.

There is a choice for writing down allowances between the straight-line method and the reducing-balance method. If the life of the asset is 18 years or more, on the reducing balance method the writing down allowance is 15 per cent and straight-line $6\frac{1}{4}$ per cent. If the life of the asset is more than 14 years but under 18 years, for reducing-balance 20 per cent, straight-line $8\frac{1}{2}$ per cent; for under 14 years, reducing-balance 25 per cent, straight-line $11\frac{1}{4}$ per cent. For industrial buildings the writing down allowance is 4 per cent per annum on a straight-line basis only.

But taxes are not due to be paid at the same time as the profit earned. This gap between earning a profit and paying tax may be significant. With a high rate of discount and a gap between one and two years this is understandable. The payment of investment grants too takes time. When the grants were first introduced the intervals between the expenditure by the applicant and the payment of the grant was eighteen months. This has since been reduced so that grants for expenditures between 1 April and 30 June 1967 were paid from 1 April 1968.

There will be no investment grant for the vehicles but assuming an initial allowance of 30 per cent, a writing down allowance of 25 per cent on the basis of reducing balance and tax payable the year after the profit is earned, our calculation becomes:

YEAR	BENEFITS (INCREASED NET REVENUE) £	TAX AT 40% £	ALLOW-ANCES £	TAX SAVED (40% OF PREVIOUS COLUMN) £	TAX PAYABLE £	CASH FLOW (BENEFITS LESS TAX PAYABLE) £
1	3000	—	5500	—2475	(—2475)	5475
2	3000	1350	1125	506	844	2156
3	3000	1350	844	380	970	2030
4	3000	1350	632	284	1066	1934
5	3000	1350	475	214	1136	1864
6	—	1350	—	—	1350	(—1350)
	1500	6750	8576	3859	2891	12 109

The allowances on the investment of £10 000 are calculated as follows:

	£	£
Year 1 Initial allowance	3000	
Writing down allowance	2500	
	5500	balance = 4500
2 Writing down	1125	3375
3 Writing down	844	2531
4 Writing down	632	1899
5 Writing down	475	1424

The cash benefits less tax must now be discounted, again assuming our acceptable discount rate of 10 per cent.

$$
\begin{array}{ll}
£ & £ \\
5475 \times 0.909 = & 4977 \\
2156 \times 0.826 = & 1781 \\
2030 \times 0.751 = & 1525 \\
1934 \times 0.683 = & 1321 \\
1864 \times 0.621 = & 1158 \\
\hline
 & 10\ 762 \\
(-1350) \times 0.564 = & (-761) \\
\hline
 & 10\ 001 \\
\hline
\end{array}
$$

The total of the discounted cash is about the same as the investment of £10 000 so the project is probably to be considered worth while. For comparison with other projects the index is

$$\frac{10\ 001}{10\ 000} \text{ or } 1.0001$$

For simplicity no account has yet been taken of the balancing allowance. In the above example, however, assuming that the vehicles were sold at the end of the fifth year for £375 each, the position would be:

57

	£
Initial outlay	10 000
Written down value	
(as "balance" above)	1 843
From sale of vehicles	1 500
Balancing allowance	343

If the resale price of the vehicles was high, say £900 each, there would have been a balancing charge as follows:

	£
Initial outlay	10 000
Written down value	
(as "balance" above)	1 843
From sale of vehicles	3 600
Balancing charge	1 757

The effect of the balancing allowance or charge is shown in the following investment case histories. What is also evident in this form of investment analysis is that for a project to be worth while it is likely that early benefits need to be substantial.

It may be argued, on the other hand, that investments with very long "lives" such as warehouses, will earn very much greater returns in two or three decades provided the post-war inflationary trend continues. Whilst this is true for one warehouse, it is not true of a number of warehouses of modern light structure which will be replaced at regular and much shorter intervals than those built by our Victorian ancestors. Replacement will usually be arranged so that there is a financial provision year by year for warehouses as for full vehicle replacement. Discounted cash flow analysis is relevant therefore. The Company transport manager may think himself lucky to have escaped the theoretical problems which beset those who advise on public works investment such as the Channel Tunnel or a new motorway or railway.

The rate of tax paid after taking grants into account and making allowances will be subject to a variety of considerations. A single rate of tax may be assumed for almost all practical purposes and the rate to be used is best discussed with the company accountant. For the purpose of our examples we will assume a tax rate of 45 per cent.

Whilst it is hardly to be expected that the transport manager will be an expert in the highly complicated situations which arise from taxation and its effect on revenue and expenditure, it is important that when making investment appraisal the general effect of taxation is understood.

The effect of taxation can be seen in the following example: assume that an investment of £10 000 for vehicles with a five-year life brings benefits in the shape of reduced costs and therefore increased net revenue of £3000 a year.

Before tax. By inspection it will be seen that the rate of return lies in the area of 15–16 per cent.

YEAR	BENEFITS (INCREASED NET REV)	DIS-COUNTED AT 15%	PRESENT VALUE	DIS-COUNTED at 16%	PRESENT VALUE
	£		£		£
1	3 000	0.870	2 610	0.862	2586
2	3 000	0.756	2 268	0.743	2229
3	3 000	0.658	1 974	0.641	1923
4	3 000	0.572	1 716	0.552	1656
5	3 000	0.497	1 491	0.476	1428
	15 000		10 059		9822

The investment was £10 000 so the discounted rate of return is between 15 and 16 per cent. To find the actual rate, take the difference between the higher and the lower present values for the discount rates that straddle the sum invested, that is £10 059 — £9822 = £237. Then take the difference between the present

59

value of the lower rate and the investment, that is £10 000 — £9822 = £178. By interpolation the rate of return is:

$$15\% + \frac{£178}{£237} = 15.74\%$$

After Tax. As there is no investment grant for the vehicles and assuming an initial allowance of 30 per cent and a writing down allowance of 25 per cent on the basis of reducing balance, our calculation is identical with that on page 57. It will be remembered that the discounted rate of return was almost exactly 10 per cent.

Corporation Tax and other tax rates will change and it is probable that the system of cash grants and allowances will also change as it has in the past. What is being attempted in this chapter is not to turn the transport manager into an accountant but to enable him to appreciate this technique and its effects when used by the accountant. It is in the area of planned investment, perhaps more than any of the other matters on which he has to make a decision, that the transport manager tends to get lost.

Investment in fork-lift trucks

As the result of a firm's rationalisation policy which involves concentration on to a smaller number of storage areas consideration is being given to the introduction of fork lift trucks. Two trucks will be required and each will cost about £5000. They are expected to last for seven years and to have a residual value of £400 each. Using the fork lifts the benefits to be gained in depot efficiency, mainly reduced handling and superior stacking of the products, is assessed to be £2000 a year. A rate of return on investment of 10 per cent is expected as a minimum.

None of the depots is in areas scheduled as Development Areas so that the investment grant on the equipment is 20 per cent. Had they been in Development Areas the grant would have been twice that. It is assumed the rate of tax for the firm is 45 per cent.

Thus the investment is the outlay of £10 000 less the grant of £2000. This grant will not be received immediately, however, and so should be discounted. The present value of the grant is therefore £2000 × 0.908 = £1818. The investment is £8182 in present values. The writing down allowance is calculated on the non-discounted investment figures of £10 000 less £2000 = £8000.

YEAR	BENEFITS (INCRE-ASED NET REVENUE) £	TAX AT 45% £	ALLOW-ANCES £	TAX SAVED (45% OF PREVIOUS COLUMN) £	TAX PAYABLE £	CASH FLOW (BENEFITS LESS TAX PAYABLE) £	DIS-COUNT AT 10%	DIS-COUNTED CASH FLOW £
1	2 000	—	2000	900	(−900)	2 900	0.909	2636
2	2 000	900	1500	675	225	1 775	0.826	1466
3	2 000	900	1125	506	394	1 606	0.751	1206
4	2 000	900	844	380	520	1 480	0.683	1011
5	2 000	900	633	285	615	1 385	0.621	860
6	2 000	900	475	214	686	1 314	0.564	741
7	2 000	900	356	160	740	1 260	0.513	646
8	—	900	—	—	900	(−900)	0.467	(−420)
	14 000	6300	—	—	—	10 820	—	8146
Residual value and balancing allowance:								
	800	—	267	120	—	920	0.467	430
	14 8000	6300	—	—	—	11 740	—	8576

Allowances are calculated as follows:
Outlay £10 000 less £2000 grant = £8000.

		£		£
Year 1	Writing down allowance	2000	balance =	6000
2	Writing down allowance	1500	balance =	4500
3	Writing down allowance	1125	balance =	3375
4	Writing down allowance	844	balance =	2531
5	Writing down allowance	633	balance =	1898
6	Writing down allowance	475	balance =	1423
7	Writing down allowance	356	balance =	1067
	Balancing allowance	267		
	Residual value			800

The discounted return on the investment covers the return required and thus the investment is considered to be a worthwhile project. To establish its priority among other projects its index is:

$$\frac{£8576}{8182} = 1.048$$

Investment in office machinery

A recommendation is made that in the dispatch and transport accounting office the introduction of machines would enable a staff reduction of one clerk to be made. Allowing for pension contributions, National Health contributions, Selective Employment Tax and other costs this would mean a saving of about £1000 a year. The machinery costs about £5000 and a reasonable life before obsolescence and the risk of unreliability would be ten years. Some of the equipment would still be useful after ten years, however, and a residual value of £500 is estimated.

YEAR	BENEFITS (INCREASED NET REVENUE)	TAX AT 45%	ALLOWANCES	TAX SAVED (45% OF PREVIOUS COLUMN)	TAX PAYABLE	CASH FLOW (BENEFITS LESS TAX PAYABLE)	DISCOUNT AT 10%	DISCOUNTED CASH FLOW
	£	£	£	£	£	£	£	£
1	1 000	—	2750	1238	(−1238)	2238	0.909	2034
2	1 000	450	563	253	197	803	0.826	663
3	1 000	450	422	190	260	740	0.751	556
4	1 000	450	316	142	308	692	0.683	473
5	1 000	450	237	107	343	657	0.621	408
6	1 000	450	178	80	370	630	0.564	355
7	1 000	450	134	60	390	610	0.513	313
8	1 000	450	100	45	405	595	0.467	278
9	1 000	450	75	34	416	584	0.424	248
10	1 000	450	56	25	425	575	0.386	222
11	—	450	—	—	450	(−450)	0.350	(−158)
	10 000	4500				7674		5392
	Residual value and Balancing charge							
	500	—	(−331)	(−149)	149	351	0.350	123
	10 500	—	—	—	—	8025	—	5515

A rate of return on investment of 10 per cent is expected as a minimum.

No grant would be available for such an investment and it is assumed the rate of tax for the firm is 40 per cent.

Allowances are calculated as follows:

		£	£
OUTLAY £5000			
Year 1	Initial allowance	1500	
	Writing down allowance	1250	
		2750	balance = 2250
2	Writing down allowance	563	balance = 1687
3	Writing down allowance	422	balance = 1265
4	Writing down allowance	316	balance = 949
5	Writing down allowance	237	Balance = 712
6	Writing down allowance	178	balance = 534
7	Writing down allowance	134	balance = 400
8	Writing down allowance	100	balance = 300
9	Writing down allowance	75	balance = 225
10	Writing down allowance	56	balance = 169
	Balancing charge	331	
	Residual value		500

The discounted return on the investment covers the return required and the mechanisation is acceptable as a project. To establish its priority among other projects its index is 1.103.

Investment in vehicles

On a threatened increase in carriers' charges and a general dissatisfaction with the service provided within a 50 miles (80.5 km) area of a works, a recommendation is made to deliver in the firm's own vehicles. Service would deteriorate as delivery schedules would be geared to delivery once a week. On the other hand, it was felt that packaging costs would be reduced and customer contact would be maintained more effectively.

A financial assessment was made of these less tangible items of the changeover to calculate the net effect of the changeover. The required five new vehicles would cost £10 000 and would last four years. The savings in carriers' charges plus the benefits deemed to accrue would be £3500 a year. They could then be sold for £300 each. A rate of return on investment of 10 per cent is expected as a minimum.

No grant would be available for such an investment and it is assumed the rate of tax for the firm is 45 per cent.

YEAR	BENEFITS (INCREA- SED NET REVENUE) £	TAX AT 45% £	ALLOW- ANCES £	TAX SAVED (45% OF PREVIOUS COLUMN) £	TAX PAYABLE £	CASH FLOW (BENEFITS LESS TAX PAYABLE) £	DIS- COUNT AT 10% £	DIS- COUNTED CASH FLOW £
1	3 500	—	5500	2475	(−2475)	5 975	0.909	5 431
2	3 500	1575	1125	506	1069	2 431	0.826	2 008
3	3 500	1575	844	380	1195	2 305	0.751	1 731
4	3 500	1575	632	284	1291	2 209	0.683	1 509
5	—	1575	—	—	1575	(−1575)	0.621	(−978)
	14 000	—	—	—	—	11 345	—	9 701
	Residual value and balancing allowance							
	1 500	—	399	180	(−180)	1 680	0.621	1 043
	15 500	—	—	—	—	13 025	—	10 744

Allowances are calculated as follows:

		£	£
OUTLAY £10 000			
Year 1	Initial allowance	3000	
	Writing down allowance	2500	
		5500	balance = 4500
2	Writing down allowance	1125	balance = 3375
3	Writing down allowance	844	balance = 2531
4	Writing down allowance	632	balance = 1899
	Balancing allowance	399	
	Residual value		1500

The discounted return on the investment covers the return required and the proposition is acceptable and ranked with other possible projects. To evaluate its priorities for this its index is:

$$\frac{£10\ 744}{10\ 000} = 1.0\ 744$$

Summary of chapter

1   Whilst the firm's investment planning will rarely be the responsibility of the transport manager he must be aware of the implications for his part of the business.

2   Traditional methods are still useful as rule-of-thumb techniques but where there exists slender margins between the decision to invest or not to invest more sophisticated techniques become necessary.

3   From most points of view the most useful technique for the transport manager is to assess annual flows of cash resulting from an investment.

4   To put future flows of cash into perspective the value of such future flows should be discounted.

5   Most firms will postulate a minimum acceptable rate of return on investment and this should be used as the present value factor or discount rate. If the benefits resulting from an investment appropriately discounted total more than the capital outlay then the investment is worth while.

6   To compare one worth-while investment with another an index may be given to the project by dividing the present values of benefits by the amount invested.

7   The implication of taxation must be considered. Consideration must be given to:
   (*a*) Investment grants.
   (*b*) Initial and writing down allowances.
   (*c*) Balancing allowances or charges.
   —and the time relationship between benefits and taxation incidence.

8   Grants vary between investment made in areas designated as Development Areas by the Board of Trade and those not so designated. In broad terms handling equipment used within a firms premises qualifies for a grant and in some cases so do industrial buildings. Lorries and cars

for business use do not. Lorries instead get a substantial investment allowance.

9   The effect of discounting the cash flow is that it is important to realise returns quickly rather than nearer the end of the life of the asset.

Assessing the value of professional carriers

One might think that it would be cheaper and safer and quicker for most goods to be handed to professional carriers for bulk carriage, inter-factory movement or distribution. Anybody in the business knows that this is not so. The growth of *C* licence fleets in post-war years has been substantial. (See Figure 5:1.) The amount of goods to be moved has also grown, but still the increase in numbers of vehicles operating on *C* licences has been in part at the expense of professional carriers.

1938	365 000
1946	383 700
1951	796 400
1956	996 200*
1961	1 216 000
1966	1 250 000
1967	1 287 000

*Of which over half under $1\frac{1}{2}$ hundredweight (127kg)

FIGURE 5:1 NUMBER OF *C* LICENCE VEHICLES
Source: *Annual Abstract of Statistics* issued by HMSO

Whilst there is one school of thought that protests that individual choice of the way in which goods are to be moved is indispensable to the dynamic development of British industry, there is another school of thought that suggests that in the overall national interest congested roads and under-used railways are a national disaster.

Anyone who has driven behind a heavy lorry in the secondary road system of this country would appreciate the advantages of transferring the contents of that lorry onto a railway train and eliminating the lorry. Unfortunately, the railway system inevitably requires road servicing at the terminals and is already considered over-extensive and poorly utilised. Despite this, many areas of the country are inadequately served.

Major private *C* licence road vehicle fleets are undoubtedly with us for the next few decades. Once a company has embarked on a policy of providing its own transport, it usually caters for those movements which are low cost per unit carried. Residual traffic is left with carriers. Deprived of the low cost movements, carriers' costs tend to rise and this in turn tempts the private vehicle owner to extend his own field of operation. If, in addition to this, the peak forwardings are at a time when the carrier is also burdened with heavy traffic from other customers, the situation is aggravated. Due to yet higher costs because of under-use of his services at off-peak times, the carrier is forced to increase his charges. Again, the customer tends to extend his *C* licence activity.

There comes a point, however, when the private vehicle operator will no longer wish to extend his network of operations because the traffic to be forwarded can no longer be economically handled. For the carrier such marginal or residual traffic is only acceptable if there are similar marginal traffics from other companies or very high unit charges are made and paid.

Thus, just as in the inter-war years the professional haulier peeled off traffic from the railway system, the characteristic of the post-war years has been the development of private carriage at the expense of both the professional haulier and the railways.

It is only reasonable, therefore, not to compare marginal charges but to make a comparison of the costs of giving carriers most, if not all, the traffic and the cost of moving most, if not all, the traffic in private vehicles. Should carriers not be able to compete on this basis, it is sensible to allocate the marginal traffic to whoever will carry it. There is a danger. If carriers are edged out of business, movements to areas which involve high unit cost operation may be left to the *C* licence vehicle.

Yet cost is not the only criterion against which a carrier or private carriage is judged. Undoubtedly one of the biggest factors contributing to the growth of the *C* licence vehicles has been that of service.

Service

Often the only indication a transport manager has of the quality of the service being provided is that of the number and nature of the complaints received by the distribution or the sales manager. It is worth while the transport manager conducting a test from time to time. Inclusion of suitably worded return business cards in packages sent out may be an appropriate method. A more direct approach, taking a random sample and writing or telephoning or even visiting recipients of goods, is perhaps better but more time-consuming and therefore more expensive. Carriers themselves can rarely be relied upon to give one the required information. Even where proof of delivery is insisted upon, the operation of linking the documentary evidence of individual deliveries on their part to the known time of tender to the customer is often laborious.

For larger units of transport within this country overnight movement is usual. Most journeys are conveniently undertaken in twelve-hour span from the close of work one day to the start of work the next day.

Whilst speed of delivery is important (because once committed to an order the sales manager is anxious to effect it as soon as possible), the quality of service may be discussed under the following headings.

Control
Control is easily effected for bulk movements in the case of road transport because a driver is with the vehicle throughout

the movement. Similarly, with train movements, a single crew might move the train from one point to another. Even when train crews are changed it is relatively difficult to misplace a train of 500–700 tons net.

Where delivery operations are concerned, however, the importance of control over orders, which could be small in size but large in value, is important. A customer's goodwill is rapidly dissipated by failure to deliver. A carrier who cannot provide a reliable and effective service is soon discarded by a manufacturer or wholesaler. The alternatives could be use of another carrier or use of private vehicles. It might be cheaper in the long run to have a high cost distribution service but to have satisfied customers providing bigger and better orders. By careful selection of carriers to different areas it might be possible to get both a satisfactory service and to get it at a modest cost.

Convenience

In order to complete their collections, carriers have to call no later than a time which enables them to return to their depot in time for the goods to be transferred into trunk vehicles, or for the vehicles themselves to be available for commencement of the trunk journey. Where orders to be met are produced late, it is sometimes convenient to have a vehicle available after normal working hours which can then be loaded away in order to meet a deadline. Need for such a facility, of course, varies from trade to trade, but in some trades the value of having a standby vehicle of this kind is very great. If it is a very high cost to provide a standby vehicle and all the facilities required to allow late loading, it could be that better production planning would remove the need for the vehicle and allow loading and dispatch in normal working hours.

Specialisation

Increasingly in modern industry, the goods to be transported require special techniques for handling and protection. These can best be provided by movement in specialised vehicles, particularly so for materials in bulk, such as fuel oil, cement, wheat, and various chemicals in powder or in liquid form. More carriers than ever are providing customers with specialised vehicles and entering into long-term contracts with customers.

Packaging

Together with specialised facilities for handling, and perhaps special vehicles, goes the advantage of experience in handling one particular commodity or range. This may allow a more modest type of packaging. Packages handed to general goods carriers will almost inevitably be conveyed with other goods. Corn flakes are not improved by loading with a proprietary lavatory cleaner and disinfectant. They may even be treated without the sense of responsibility that a private vehicle and staff might adopt. But carriers too are specialising in types of goods.

Claims

It is usual for carriers to limit their liability for claims for loss and damage:

1   To a sum of £800 a ton on the gross weight of the consignment.
2   Where the loss is in respect of part of a consignment, only in the same proportion as the partial loss is to the whole of the consignment.
3   Not less than £10 in respect of any one consignment.

Normally liability for loss or damage would not be accepted if there were insufficient or improper packing or labelling.

The carrier usually demands that he must be advised in writing within three days and a claim must be made out within seven days of the end of the transit where there is damage or pilferage. For total loss or non-delivery, advice must be within twenty-eight days and a claim made within forty-two days after the commencement of transit. Where carriers have parcels in their possession in transit for as much as two or three weeks,

71

the time allowed is not excessive nor, on some occasions, even adequate.

Sundays and bank holidays are not included in the days to be calculated and a claim is not necessarily invalidated if it is not reasonably possible for the customer to make the claim in writing. These are, however, stringent conditions. It is impossible in some businesses (mail order is a good example) to hope to meet such conditions always. If special arrangements cannot be made this could prove an embarrassment.

Dangerous goods are sometimes not accepted at all by carriers—where they are accepted they are subject to separate conditions of carriage and sometimes with severe penalties if there is damage to property or injury to persons.

The Road Haulage Association's standard set of "conditions of carriage" are set out in detail in Appendix 1.

Because of the incidence of claims especially where goods are of high value, an attempt is sometimes made to cover through an insurance company. Where this is the practice because of unfortunate claims experience, the insurance company tends to seek high premiums. It is usually more satisfactory to undertake a vigorous campaign of investigation of claims and careful carrier selection.

Prestige or sales value

It is always difficult to assess how much importance should be attributed to the advantages of having a spick and span fleet. Some breweries insist on delivering some of their products by horse and cart. Some retail stores have an old-fashioned type of vehicle which has become easily identifiable with that firm. All this is part of "image" building. Undoubtedly this has an important part to play in the marketing of a firm's products.

Perhaps more important, however, is the relationship between drivers and customers. Many firms use drivers as a regular contact with customers and drivers are responsible for the collection of orders and the preservation of goodwill. This sometimes militates against the careful planning and disciplined operation introduced by the transport manager. The people who control purchasing at a firm are not always the same as those responsible for acceptance of goods. Time may therefore be lost in taking documents or an order book from the reception bay to the purchasing office. If this also involves leaving a vehicle unattended with valuable goods on it, there is another risk involved. Nevertheless, the relationship which develops between drivers and customers can help in the promotion of good trading relations.

Strike risk

In a world where the nationalised transport organisations, especially those linked with the railway, have not yet succeeded in the elimination of both local and country-wide industrial unrest, there are few users of transport who do not link their affairs with more than one transport provider if this is possible. The publicity given to strikes in nationalised undertakings is often excessive. Nevertheless where there are likely to be labour troubles and withdrawal of services the consequences of having no contacts elsewhere could be serious.

Quantification of service benefits

Too little attempt is made to evaluate these service benefits. Whilst evaluation can never be precise, the progress made in the technique of "social benefit" costing used in the economic studies of road building and elsewhere gives clues to the ways in which estimates may be made.

To measure anything there must be at least one alternative. Having made the choice, the cost of one solution is that of not having the other. Thus it is unwise to suggest, as is frequently the case, that we need the good relationship established between a driver and a customer without mention of the cost. If a more impersonal service of equal efficiency were established would the customer be as valuable? It is worth while from time to time making evaluations along these lines.

It is worth evaluating, for example, the cost of allowing orders to be sent down for vehicles after the normal process of handling at the dispatch bay and loading of vehicles has begun. The disorganisation which late orders can cost the firm through transport rearrangement is often ignored. If a load needs to be rearranged this involves a handling cost which can be measured in terms of overtime payments. If the load cannot be rearranged but the vehicle has to be rerouted, this again can be measured. If the late order is not accepted will the customer withdraw his custom or not? If he does, how much would the loss of his custom affect the profitability of the enterprise? Would the cessation of orders from such a customer enable greater reliability to be given to the dispatch of orders to other customers?

All these questions are answerable only with reference to a particular circumstance. The loss caused by stopped production can be calculated if a vehicle with raw materials or semi-finished goods fails to arrive on time. Obviously answers can rarely be provided without a great deal of investigation. This investigation could not of course be continuous but from time to time is probably well worth doing. It is a good thing to show the empiricists a few facts.

Keeping costs down

Movement in bulk

The costs of using carriers are the charges made by the carriers for the service provided. In the case of raw material inputs or semi-finished products where bulk movements are concerned, either the whole traffic is allotted to a carrier for him to arrange movement or the control is exercised by the firm concerned and the operation is divided between a number of carriers. Charges for this sort of operation are usually arrived at in a private deal between the carrier and the manager concerned. From the carrier's point of view, there are advantages in having a long-term agreement. Such a commitment will allow him to arrange the disposition of his equipment to maximum advantage. This should mean reduced costs and should therefore be reflected in the price charged. Should such a long-term arrangement be agreed, then the agreement might incorporate an escalation clause. The carrier is thus able to avoid the yearly or twice-yearly trek to customers to agree new charges for services supplied in an economy subject to inflationary tendencies. Carriers do not always get the increases they seek and the time and effort consumed in negotiation are often expensive.

An escalation clause is designed to relate the charges made for the service to the expenditures the carrier has to make in providing the service or to more general price levels. Such an arrangement should not be unfair to either contracting party. An index must be chosen to which the charge will be related. The carrier would in most cases prefer an index which is likely to increase at a greater rate than cost. The user of the service on the other hand, prefers an index which will rise at a lesser rate. It is arguable, for example, that if the index is related to wage increases in a labour intensive industry where there are too many staff employed for economic efficiency, then by using such an index the contract helps perpetuate inefficiency. If, on the other hand, an index of prices is used, this may have little relevance to the provision of transport.

The two most usual indices which are found to be acceptable to both sides are the wholesale price index and the retail price index. These are published by Her Majesty's Stationary Office and are therefore unlikely to be affected by changes in calculation without due warning. They are, however, subject from time to time to revision and such revisions would affect charges. It is therefore wise to establish that the figures published in the monthly Digest of Statistics are to be accepted and that the adjustments will be made at agreed times each year and in retrospect and an allowance made for the retrospective amount. Because the indexes are produced four months after the event this is important where large amounts are at stake. An appropriate starting point should be selected with care if an index is subject to seasonal fluctuations.

The trend of one set of retail and one set of wholesale price indices are shown in Figures 5:2–3.

Where large bulk movements are involved it is fairly easy for both sides to appreciate the amount of equipment necessary, the joint costs which must be shared with other traffics and

1962	101.6
3	103.6
4	107.0
5	112.1
6	116.5
7	119.4

(Base: 16 January 1962 = 100)

FIGURE 5:2   RETAIL PRICE INDEX

Source: *Monthly Digest of Statistics* issued by HMSO

1962	118.6
3	119.9
4	123.9
5	129.6
6	133.2
7	134.9

(Base: 1954 = 100)

FIGURE 5:3   WHOLESALE PRICE INDEX

Source: *Monthly Digest of Statistics* issued by HMSO

also to allow over and above this an element for indirect costs and for management. Most big deals are the result of careful costing on both sides. Whilst it might not be possible always for a firm to produce its own service at a price which is nearly competitive, it is sometimes possible to take over part of the service. For example, one might reduce charges by buying one's own wagons and maintaining them. This can either be through purchase outright or by renting from hire firms.

The agreed unit of charge can also have significance. Conventionally, for bulk movements, the charge is raised per ton. As we have seen, however, the unit of cost is not per ton. In the case of the road vehicle it is the vehicle. In the case of the railway it is either the train or the wagon. The charges therefore would be related only in the loosest fashion to the cost of the vehicle or vehicles provided. The transport manager is only prepared to pay if he cannot get the job done more cheaply by anyone else and if the service is satisfactory. No matter what

TRAFFIC	TRAFFIC RECEIPT	COST DIRECTLY AFFECTED BY FLUCTUATIONS OF TRAFFIC—FUEL, OIL, TYRES, ETC	BALANCE	COSTS ONLY AFFECTED JOINTLY THROUGH FLUCTUATIONS OF A GROUP OF TRAFFIC FOR EXAMPLE: DRIVERS LICENCES	BALANCE	COSTS AFFECTED EVEN MORE JOINTLY FOR EXAMPLE: VEHICLES, WASHING, MAINTENANCE ETC	BALANCE	OVERHEADS COSTS FOR EXAMPLE: ADMINISTRATIVE, GENERAL MANAGER
(a)	250	100	150	150	50		50	
(b)	100	50	50		100	100		
(c)	450	250	200	200	50		50	100
(d)	250	150	100		50			
(e)	150	100	50	150	50	50	50	
(f)	350	200	150		50			
(g)	500	300	200	200	50		50	
(h)	200	150	50					
	£2250	£1300		£700		£150		£100

If joint and overhead cost were allocated in proportion to the direct costs of each traffic the following situation would result:

TRAFFIC	RECEIPTS	COSTS DIRECTLY AFFECTED	PROPORTIONATE ALLOCATION OF OTHER COSTS	TOTAL COSTS
	£	£	£	£
(a)	250	100	73	173
(b)	100	50	37	87
(c)	450	250	182	432
(d)*	250	150	110	260
(e)*	150	100	73	173
(f)	350	200	146	346
(g)*	500	300	219	519
(h)*	200	150	110	260
	£2250	£1300	£950	£2250

FIGURE 5:4. HYPOTHETICAL SITUATION OF REVENUE AND DIRECT AND INDIRECT COSTS

unit the charge is based on, the carrier will attempt to maximise the value of his competitive advantage where it exists. Cross-subsidisation of one traffic by another is rarely possible on a massive scale, but provided all costs directly attributable to the traffic are covered, it is not necessarily against the interests of the customer or the carrier (or for that matter of the economy as a whole) if one traffic is subsidised by another for other costs.

The situation may be illustrated by examining a hypothetical situation where eight traffics are carried. Hypothetical costs and revenues are shown in Figure 5:4.

In this situation every traffic covers those costs directly attributable and in total all traffics cover all the costs of the enterprise. But, after taking away the directly attributable costs, the contributions to other costs incurred by the business are not the same from each traffic. If a system of charges were introduced to make it so, the situation might arise that because of competition some traffic would no longer be carried. Costs other than direct will, of course, remain because of the existence of the remaining traffics.

If joint and overhead costs, that is all costs except those directly affected by fluctuations of a particular traffiic are allocated in proportion to the direct costs, then only substantial margins of profit or non-competitive situations can prevent financial disaster. Yet this is not an uncommon practice. In such a case, traffics (*d*), (*e*) (*g*), and (*h*) (see these letters marked* in Figure 5:4) would not be carried. Thus whilst £1100 receipts would be lost the savings in cost would amount to only £900. A redistribution of the costs other than direct over the remaining traffics would make them less profitable to carry.

A situation could then arise where a previously satisfactory commercial position is changed to a substantial loss-making situation.

This situation is sometimes recognised in the offer by carriers to provide a two-part tariff. The first part of the tariff is a lump sum payment, annually or spread out over the year. This payment is designed to cover those costs which can be reasonably allocated to this traffic as a whole but not to particular movements. There is then an additional charge per ton which covers running costs or those which could be directly related to particular movements. The additional charge per ton is thus of course lower than it would have been had the charge per ton been burdened with a proportion of indirect cost.

If it is possible for the traffic to be increased there is a direct incentive to the firm to make greater use of this particular carrier. The marginal unit is cheap. From the point of view of the provider of the service, there is equally a safeguard against the diminution of traffic. Should the traffic reduce, the unit cost when both parts of the two-part tariff are taken into account obviously grows. Such a two-part tariff is illustrated in Figure 5:5.

Assuming that in the situation of Figure 5:4 the tonnage carried was 2250 tons and there was considerable scope or development of services without increase of joint or overhead costs. A two-part tariff could be as follows:

Part 1
A single period payment of £950
(which may be staged)

Part 2
A payment of 11s 6d (£0.57½) a ton carried
(this charge must cover direct costs)

The effect of varying tonnages on the two-part tarriff would be

TONNAGE CARRIED	1000 TONS £	2250 TONS £	3500 TONS £
Part 1 Charge	950	950	950
Part 2 Charge	575	1295	2015
TOTAL	1525	2245	2965
Average charge a ton	£1-10-6 (£.52½)	£1	17s (£0.85)

FIGURE 5:5   EXAMPLE OF A TWO-PART TARIFF

Distribution

The relationship between cost and charge is much more tenuous when considering the distribution activities of carriers.

THE VALUE OF PROFESSIONAL CARRIERS

Because the business is made up of a large number of customers offering varying amounts of traffic at varying times from and to different places, it is usual for carriers to prepare a list of charges.

The scales of charges are generally produced from a standing charge per consignment or package and a progression charge which varies with mileage. Charges for some standard consignment sizes for British Road Services, British Rail, and a public road carrier are shown in Figure 5:6.

It will be seen that the cheapest way of sending an 11 pound package to Accrington from Leicester is by British Rail's passenger service. For a 28 pound (12.7 kg) package, however, the cheapest way of dispatch is by National Carriers Limited.

	CONSIGNMENT SIZE			
	11 POUNDS (5 kg)	28 POUNDS (12.7 kg)	56 POUNDS (25.4 kg)	3 HUNDRED-WEIGHT (152.4 kg)
British Rail parcels by passenger service	5s 6d (£0.27½)	12s (£0.60)	19s 6d (£0.97½)	£3-17-10 (£3.89)
National Carriers	6s 6d (£0.32½)	6s 6d (£0.32½)	9s (£0.45)	£1-0-0 (£1)
British Road Services General tariff	6s 8d (£0.33½)	10s 1d (£0.50½)	13s 6d (£0.67½)	£2-1-10 (£2.09)
Trade tariff	6s (0.30)	8s 4d (£0.41½)	11s 4d (£0.56½)	£1-15-1 (£1.75½)
Exceptional tariff	6s (£0.30)	8s 3d (£0.41)	10s 5d (£0.52)	£1-12-3 (£1.61)
Carrier A Standard tariff	8s 3d (£0.41)	8s 3d (£0.41)	11s 8d (£0.58½)	£1-19-4 (£1.96½)
Exceptional tariff	7s 6d (£0.37½)	7s 6d (£0.37½)	10s 3d (£0.51)	£1-15-11 (£1.79½)
Carrier B Standard	7s 3d (£0.36)	10s 9d (£0.54)	14s 3d (£0.71)	£2-11-3 (£2.56)
Carrier C Standard	9s 8d (£0.48½)	9s 8d (£0.48½)	14s 4d (£0.71½)	£2-16-4 (£2.81½)
Exceptional	8s 10d (£0.44)	8s 10d (£0.44)	12s 10d (£0.64)	£2-11-2 (£2.56)
General Post Office	7s 6d (£0.37½)			

FIGURE 5:6   COMPARISON OF CARRIERS' CHARGES

Example based on collection in Leicester and delivery in Accrington of goods with a bulk not considered excessive in relation to weight.

80

For this particular movement National Carriers remains the cheapest for consignment weights of 56 pounds (25.4 kg) and 3 hundredweight (152.4 kg).

However, carriers tend to select the areas to which they will carry cheaply so that they can maximise the throughput and thus minimise unit costs. British Rail and National Carriers charge much more for collection and delivery in green field areas away from the more urban centres of population. Charges vary too when surcharges for carriage of certain goods and for bulkiness are taken into account. Charges may also be much higher if a consignment is passed on to another carrier and a separate additional charge is made.

Service advantages may outweigh marginal differences in cost. Here again the user must be selective. On trunk routes some of BR's services are first class. On others they are not. When some private road carriers hand consignments to a third party it is known for the service to deteriorate. Some carriers seem to take more care of goods than others. Some seem prepared to adjust to a user's needs more quickly than others.

The most common unit for a transport charge is the consignment. This is sensible, as the costs of tendering the goods or collecting the goods have the most marked influence on the profitability of most enterprises dealing with small consignments or parcels. It is the number of places to be visited rather than the number of parcels to be delivered at any one place that is important when small consignments are concerned. It is almost as easy to tender three parcels as it is to tender one. A transport manager who accepts a per package charge must be very sure of what he is about.

When considering the charges of different carriers, the levels at which charges change are important. British Rail freight services, for example, have a minimum weight of 28 pounds (12.7 kg) a consignment. BRS have a minimum weight of 7 pounds (3.2 kg) a consignment. British Rail passenger services have a minimum of 8 pounds (3.6 kg). Other carriers have various minima. The groupings of weight of consignments over the consignment size range can also be surprisingly significant. Judicious choice of carrier can materially affect costs if the average weight per consignment is more favourable by one schedule of charges than another. This is illustrated in Figure 5:7.

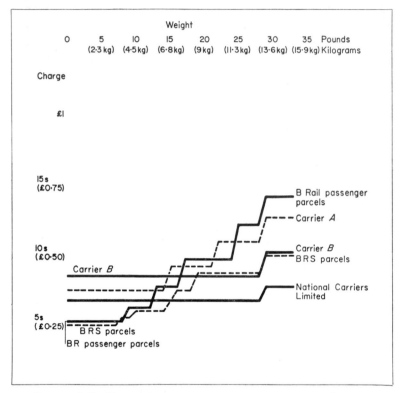

FIGURE 5:7   EFFECT OF WEIGHT GROUPINGS ON CARRIERS' CHARGES

It will be seen from Figure 5:7 that the BRS or the passenger train services is cheapest for smaller parcels whilst the private road carriers and National Carriers tend to become competitive for rather larger consignments, provided they service the particular destination desired.

Reductions in charges are sometimes offered to customers making extensive use of small parcels services. This is either in the form of a discount at the end of the account or by allowing use of a separate scale of charges at a lower level.

In order to save accountancy work for the carrier and the user, some years ago the flat rate of charge became popular. This is an arrangement whereby the traffic is tested at normal rates, an average charge is agreed between the user and the provider of the service and thereafter until the situation is again reviewed this charge is applied to every consignment no matter what its destination or weight. The unit of charge may be either the ton, a consignment, or a package. In order, however, to guarantee that the arrangement is fair, there is normally an undertaking that all the business, perhaps with certain specified reservations, will be handed to the carrier. Having guaranteed a specific volume of traffic, however, the user of the flat rate is in a strong position to claim that this continued commitment should bring cost benefits to the carrier and this should be reflected in a discount to him.

Carriage by air is sometimes regarded as a rather separate operation. Insofar as the time saved on the trunk movement is not dissipated at terminals (a common enough fault), the advantages of less working capital being required and the need for possibly less parking are demonstrable. Equally, where air freight is used for overseas delivery, tranship of goods may be avoided. But the charges are still high. Air freight is still, despite protestations to the contrary, an operation best suited to the transport of highly perishable goods or goods of high value for long distances and especially so where sea crossings are involved.

Awareness of changes

It is difficult for a manager to operate a large fleet of his own and deal currently with all the problems which arise with distribution and raw material movement. It is not unusual, as a result, for carriers to make a good impression with their service and price and thereafter to remain with the firm when these justifications have disappeared. To minimise the cost of distribution by public carriers, there needs to be a constant awareness of the changes in service and in pricing. Not only do units of charge change and levels of charge alter, but so do the attitudes towards discount and the ways in which this may be secured.

83

It is worth while from time to time to institute a review of the distribution arrangements with the object of minimising cost without allowing service to deteriorate. This is not, alas, a job for a new entrant to the organisation, for it requires patience and skill. Quite small differences in unit charge are significant when it is remembered that medium size firms will often spend £50 000–£100 000 a year on transport and that this involves as much as 500 packages a day.

Case histories

From road carrier to rail

A steel company in South Wales moved finished steel to stockists in the Midlands. Goods were moved in 16-ton capacity road vehicles which were contracted specifically to the steel company and managed by a private company. The vehicles provided a next-morning delivery and were able to secure a large number of return loads to South Wales. The charge for carrying the steel was 26 shillings (£1.30) a ton. Under a new and vigorous steel company management, the position was reviewed.

Tenders were asked from others to ascertain alternatives. British Rail offered to supply three times weekly or nightly a train capable of carrying 450 tons which would be available for loading each day in the firm's private siding. The train would run overnight to the Midlands and the steel would be delivered by road the following morning, in much the same way as the former pattern. The charge, inclusive of delivery for the train load, was £450.

Because the train was operated regularly and the delivery services provided exclusively for the steel, a satisfactory service was provided by the railways and this matched the previous service by the hauliers. In addition if maximum use were made of the train capacity, the cost per ton could be as low as £1. In fact, maximum capacity was not always used but on average there was a reduction from the 26 shillings (£1.30) previously charged. Annual cost reduction for about 100 000 tons came to about £15 000.

Certain adjustments had to be made at the firm's premises to meet the demands of rail loading rather than road loading, but this was compensated for by the fact that rail wagons could stand all day whereas road vehicles had to be scheduled in and out. The steel company also benefited from the opportunity to use larger trains for which the railways planned to charge only slightly more and which would therefore reduce the conveyance charge.

From own fleet to carrier

A firm producing a refined and processed raw material decided to reduce its heavy investment in its own vehicles. A scale of charges was produced for movement from the various factories to the relatively small number of consumers of the product and this was offered to operators of large vehicles known to be interested. Commitments were made to guarantee minimum consignments over a long period and firms were invited to provide suitable vehicles. In some cases a financial interest was taken in the firm concerned to provide the necessary capital immediately required.

Efficiency was secured because the operators knew their income from a given amount of work and operated within that framework. The operators pressed for rapid loading and a large number of journeys. Standing time of vehicles at factories was immediately reduced. In their own interest, the operators sorted out their own difficulties and what had been major management problems over a large fleet were cut down to size. This benefit was in addition to the reduced capital investment which was itself worth many thousands of pounds a year.

Rail and carrier combination

A large firm distributing clothing to shops and warehouses was completely dependent on the British Rail passenger/parcels service. An exercise was conducted to examine alternatives. Whilst some of the passenger services were first class and over-all a substantial deduction from standard charges had been agreed, selective use of other carriers in conjunction with the railway service produced considerable benefits.

From LEICESTER to:	BR PASSENGER PARCELS SERVICE 8 pounds (3.63 kg)	56 pounds (25.4 kg)	NATIONAL CARRIERS LTD 8 pounds (3.63 kg)	56 pounds (25.4 kg)	BRS PARCELS 8 pounds (3.63 kg)	56 pounds (25.4 kg)
LONDON	5s (£0.25)	19s 6d (£0.97½)	6s 6d (£0.32½)	9s (£0.45)	5s 1d (£0.25½)	10s 8d (£0.53½)
SOUTHEND-ON-SEA	5s (£0.25)	£1 1s (£1.05)	7s (£0.35)	10s (£0.50)	5s 4d (£0.26½)	12s 1d (£0.60½)
HOLYHEAD	5s 6d (£0.27½)	£1 2s (£1.10)	8s 6d (£0.42½)	11s (£0.55)	No direct service	
BIRMINGHAM	5s (£0.25)	18s (£0.90)	6s (£0.30)	7s (£0.35)	5s 1d (£0.25½)	9s (£0.45)
GLASGOW	6s (£0.30)	£1 7s 6d (£1.37½)	10s 6d (£0.52½)	13s 6d (£0.67½)	5s 7d (£0.28)	15s 4d (£0.76½)
KIRCUDBRIGHT	7s (£0.35)	£1 12s (£1.60)	13s (£0.65)	18s 6d (£0.92½)	5s 7d (£0.28)	14s 8d (£0.73½)
BRISTOL	5s (£0.25)	19s 6d (£0.97½)	6s 6d (£0.32½)	9s (£0.45)	5s 4d (£0.26½)	11s 7d (£0.58)
ST IVES	6s (£0.30)	£1 8s (£1.40)	11s (£0.55)	14s 6d (£0.72½)	5s 7d (£0.28)	15s 4d (£0.76½)
LIVERPOOL	5s (£0.25)	19s 6d (£0.97½)	6s 6d (£0.32½)	9s (£0.45)	5s 4d (£0.26½)	11s 4d (£0.56½)
WEST KIRBY	5s 6d (£0.27½)	£1 2s (£1.10)	8s 6d (£0.42½)	11s (£0.55)	5s 7d (£0.28)	11s 10d (£0.59)

From LEICESTER to:	CARRIER A 8 pounds (3.63 kg)	56 pounds (25.4 kg)	CARRIER B 8 pounds (3.63 kg)	56 pounds (25.4 kg)
LONDON	6s (£0.30)	10s 6d (£0.52½)	7s 5d (£0.37)	10s 1d (£0.50½)
SOUTHEND-ON-SEA	6s (£0.30)	11s 3d (£0.56)	No direct service	
HOLYHEAD	7s 9d (£0.39)	16s 3d (£0.81)	No direct service	
BIRMINGHAM	5s 9d (£0.29)	9s 9d (£0.49)	4s 9d (£0.24)	8s 11d (£0.44½)
GLASGOW	7s (£0.35)	16s 9d (£0.84)	10s 9d (£0.54)	16s 2d (£0.81)
KIRCUDBRIGHT	8s 3d (£0.41)	18s 3d (£0.91)	10s 9d (£0.54)	16s 2d (£0.81)
BRISTOL	6s (£0.30)	11s 3d (£0.56)	8s (£0.40)	11s 2d (£0.56)
ST IVES	8s 6d (£0.42½)	£1 0s 6d (£1.02½)	10s 9d (£0.54)	16s 2d (£0.81)
LIVERPOOL	6s (£0.30)	11s 3d (£0.56)	8s 7d (£0.43)	12s 3d (£0.61)
WEST KIRBY	7s 5d (£0.37)	14s 3d (£0.71)	8s 3d (£0.41)	11s 8d (£0.58½)

FIGURE 5.8 EFFECT OF DESTINATION ON CARRIERS' CHARGES

As an illustration of the scope available to such an organisation, the following example may be quoted. Ten selected destinations (seven of which are in main towns and three of which are in out-of-the-way areas) are shown and the range of charges available is indicated.

It will be seen that to London the cheapest service is by rail. To Kirkcudbright in Scotland the cheapest service is by road. Choice of carrier to other destinations if a road service is preferred varies from place to place. Obviously there could be difficulty sorting to a large number of carriers so there would be advantage in using carriers who provide a satisfactory service to an area at a reasonable cost.

Summary of chapter

1   The growth of *C* licence fleets indicates that professional carriers cannot always provide the right service at the right price.

2   The services of professional carriers may be compared to own vehicle use in terms of: cost, convenience, specialisation, packaging, claims, prestige or sales value and strike risk.

3   Charges for input or inter-factory movement by professional carriers are usually negotiated.

4   Charges for input or inter-factory movement are usually shown per ton.

5   Distribution charges, because they are usually for smaller consignments, are normally related to a tariff.

6   There is a trend to "package" deals for distribution, namely agreed flat rates or single payments per period.

7   Case histories emphasise the unreality of marginal measures being employed when decisions are taken about use of carriers. The distribution or input problem needs review as a whole.

Hiring fleets
and choosing vehicles

The advantages (and the disadvantages) of fleet ownership can be enjoyed without investment. There are a number of firms, including a nationalised organisation, which are anxious that users should hire vehicles from them.

Benefits of hiring

The obvious advantage of hiring instead of buying vehicles is that capital is left available either for those other activities where hiring arrangements are not as readily available or for working funds. At a time when commercial banks are reducing credit facilities for working capital and hardening their arrangements on specific loans, and at a time when capital is difficult to obtain on the open market, the use of hiring arrangements becomes particularly advantageous. In addition, hiring offers many benefits.

Professional advice

The firm hiring the vehicles is often prepared to give advice on the sort of vehicle best suited to the user's needs. Some firms offering contract hire arrangements even go so far as to suggest they will act as consultants to determine possible solutions of a firm's problems. But there is always a danger in accepting advice from a party with a vested interest.

Just as a carrier will be tempted to offer a solution which involves use of his vehicle or his services, so will a vehicle leasing firm be inclined to offer a solution which involves a contract to hire its vehicles. If a particular type of vehicle is available and the contract is relatively short term, it might even be a temptation to advise use of that particular sort of vehicle. If the firm's maintenance facilities are geared to one make of vehicle and the leasing arrangement involves maintenance, it might be persuaded to suggest that from a "professional" point of view this particular vehicle, which happened to be available, is the one most suited to the user's need. Of course, this may not be so.

Temporary replacements

Where small numbers of vehicles are in use it is often difficult to arrange for vehicles to be released other than at weekends for maintenance. If vehicles are leased, however, the leasing company may arrange for replacement vehicles to be available. This also avoids the high cost of hiring on a casual basis as the result of a vehicle failure on the road or an accident.

Maintenance service

A maintenance arrangement can often be incorporated in the deal which saves a firm the trouble of either negotiating with a garage to provide servicing or providing men, equipment and materials and accommodation themselves.

Hired drivers

Contracts may be arranged with or without provision of drivers. If drivers are provided, the problems associated with the management of a team of independent and highly skilled operators are eliminated.

Hiring and discounted cash flow

The use of DCF techniques for the estimation of the advantage of entering a contracting arrangement for the hire of vehicles may be illustrated by the following example.

The project must be assessed first as a proposition for invest-ment and then as a proposition for hire.

Assume that the vehicles which were considered for purchase in the case histories outlined in Chapter 5 are obtainable by hire from one of the companies in this country offering to hire vehicles. The vehicles cost £2000 each and five were needed. They would last for four years and have a residual value of £300 each. The benefits were estimated at £3500 a year from the reduced packaging, better customer contact and more reliable though less frequent service.

Taking into account an assumed rate of tax of 45 per cent the cash flow over the period came to £13 025 and discounted at 10 per cent this reduced to £10 744. Bearing in mind the outlay of £10 000 the project had a higher index of 1.074.

If the vehicles were hired there would of course be no cash outlay. But the hire payments must be met. Assume the hire payments on the five vehicles to be £3000 annually.

YEAR	SAVED HIRE PAYMENTS £	TAX ON HIRE £	SAVED NET PAYMENTS £
1	3000		3000
2	3000	1350	1650
3	3000	1350	1650
4	3000	1350	1650
		1350	(−1350)

In addition to the tax saved on the hire payments, however, the firm would have had the benefit of the capital allowances and any residual value, both now denied it and both accruing to the hire firm. The position is therefore:

YEAR	HIRE PAYMENT SAVED £	TAX AT 45% £	ALLOW-ANCES £	TAX SAVED £	TAX PAYABLE £	CASH FLOW (BENEFITS LESS TAX PAYABLE) £	DIS-COUNT AT 10% £	DIS-COUNTED CASH FLOW £
1	3000	—	5500	2475	(−2475)	5475	0.909	4976
2	3000	1350	1125	506	844	2156	0.826	1781
3	3000	1350	844	380	970	2030	0.751	1526
4	3000	1350	632	284	1066	1934	0.683	1321
5	—	1350	—	—	1350	(−1350)	0.621	(−838)
	12 000	—	—	—	—	10 245	—	8766
	Residual value and balancing allowance							
	1 500	—	399	180	(−180)	1680	0.621	1043
	13 500	—	—	—	—	11 925	—	9809

The discounted cash flow is £11 504 and the profitability index is:

$$\frac{£\ 9809}{£10\ 000} = 0.9809$$

The proposition to lease is just about worth-while and will be ranked in order of preference with other projects, so that the cash not spent may be released for investment elsewhere in the business, provided the return on such investment is greater and has a profitability index of more than 0.9809.

Petrol economies

Whether the fleet is the result of private investment or the result of a contractual arrangement, the company can usually buy fuel and lubricants on favourable terms as fleet owners. Perhaps the most satisfactory arrangement for fuel is to dispense it to vehicles from one's own pump. The initial cost of the pump and the cost of the land required for the safeguard of this useful but potentially dangerous piece of equipment might be offset by a discount per gallon. The discount allowed should almost be the equivalent of the profit margin allowed on the fuel dispensed through the public petrol stations. The companies supplying the fuel will be conscious of possible economies in their supply arrangement. Better terms will thus be obtained if the pump is at an easily accessible point and the supply required is regular and in convenient quantities. The units of supply would be determined by the capacity of the motor vehicle tank or the rail tank used.

Discounts may also be obtained from bulk purchases generally. Not only does this apply to fuel but also to tyres and sometimes spare parts.

Drawbacks of hiring

On the other hand, it is an obvious disadvantage of leasing vehicles instead of owning them that the providers of the vehicles will expect a reasonable return from the capital they invest. They will not engage in activities where there is not a satisfactory profit. If this profit is the return due to highly efficient management of an activity or is the result of large-scale economies which could not be achieved unless the vehicles were hired to a large number of customers, then individual hirers of vehicles will be happy to pay. It is evident that this is not always so.

Inadequate service

There are cases where hirers of vehicles have not been satisfied with the service received. Excuses are offered for vehicles which are badly maintained or which are not available at specified times. Substitute vehicles of inferior size or design are not always acceptable. When a decision is being taken about the hire of vehicles, the character of the intended operation and attitude towards service should be taken into account. It could be cheaper in the case of general utility vehicles to go to a third party for an occasional vehicle on hire for a short period rather than to commit oneself to a long-term obligation merely to guard against something that might never happen.

Staff problems

If drivers are provided under the leasing arrangements, they do not always identify themselves with the interests of the hirer. If only vehicles are provided, drivers of a firm sometimes lose that pride which they develop if they have a vehicle recognisably their own. The fleet also has to be managed.

Contract terms

The terms of the contract will depend on the wishes of the lessor and lessee and are variable provided they are legally enforceable and fall within the scope of such financial regulations as exist. Contracts available may be grouped as follows:

1   Leasing of vehicles only. This is not confined to road vehicles, for railway tanks and barges are also available. In particular, oil and chemical companies have large fleets of specialised rail vehicles.

2   Contracts providing vehicles and drivers.

In both cases the charges clearly must be on a time basis with a mileage charge added. Maintenance may or may not be included in the arrangement. If it is, it would probably be computed on a mileage basis. Fuel is usually paid for separately. Cleaning and garaging of vehicles are sometimes included as part of a contract.

In fact, a firm in most cases pays on a "cost plus" basis. Variations to this general attitude of "cost plus" are found. Vehicles may be provided per journey or per day; charges may be raised against a schedule or prices per consignment, per ton or per vehicle, these charges themselves varying with mileage covered and time used.

There is a danger that unless the charges are based on a reasonable criterion, and one can imagine the difficulties in compiling such a charging system, then the dangers of "cost plus" charging will lead to operating inefficiency. It is desirable to use a system where there is a built-in incentive to efficiency. No matter how responsible the operator, there is a danger that, without an incentive, he would not maximise his effort.

Price levels

It has been known for vehicles bearing the livery of well-known companies—but actually operating on hire at a price schedule for work done—to be stopped for roadside checks and found to have, for example, bald tyres. In such a situation, of course, the lessor sometimes complains that the company to which he hires the vehicle does not allow an adequate return to him to enable proper maintenance. The users of the vehicle equally can complain that it is up to the lessor, who is not obliged to work at these charges.

In these cases the charge might have been fixed by the using company. If the lessor wishes to secure work for his company, he is forced to accept it. Much more often, the price fixers are the lessors themselves and margins of return per vehicle are established empirically.

Those firms which need only a few vehicles on hire tend to pay the highest prices. It is perhaps unfortunate that such firms are usually least able to make out a strong case in negotiation. In long-term contractual arrangement an escalation clause may be incorporated.

Choosing the vehicle

When choosing the sort of vehicles to be used, the following considerations must be taken into account.

1   Is the vehicle to be rigid or articulated? Each has its advantages on trunk operations.
2   Is the body to be a flat deck, a van or of special design?
3   Is the engine power of the vehicle sufficient for the operations envisaged, bearing in mind the nature of the axle ratios and the gearbox?
4   Is it possible to conform to the regulations about brakes, axle loadings, tyres, and weight distribution?

Roughly one third of all sales of commercial vehicles in this country are vans with a payload of under half a ton. Another third has a payload of between 10 hundredweight and 1 ton. (508 kg and 1.01 t). The rest are with a payload of over a ton. Those vehicles sold to carry a payload of 2 tons (2.02 t) number under 100 000.

The smallest vans range from the BMC mini-van to those produced by Bedfords and Fords and it is difficult to draw the line between their use as cars and as commercial vehicles.

The bigger vans require consideration of access to the load, maximum floor space, east of driver access and egress, the ability to "walk-through" to the load without dismounting and opening the tail doors and so on. Surprisingly little progress has yet been made in the installation of automatic transmission but this is coming. Often the need is to carry goods bulky in relation to weight and maximum space is an advantage. Mounting engines as far forward as possible and to the sides helps. A vehicle may need a flat decked body for palletised loads. On the other hand if palletised loads are not carried and the body floor is dropped around the wheels, a shape known as dropside, the extra capacity available can reach 15–20 per cent.

The rule for really heavy lorries has become a tractive unit or tractor and a trailer or trailers. Generally a tractor will require the use of two or more trailers and will cover 50 000 miles or more in a year. In these conditions initial price becomes less important and reliability becomes extremely important as was outlined in Chapter 2. The trailers which are relatively cheap compared to the tractor can be detached and allowed to stand whilst the expensive haulage unit is moved on to another trailer for a journey. Detachable trailers have operational advantages for smaller vehicles too.

For the small van market the field is dominated by BMC and Fords. For the medium vans most users turn to Bedfords, Fords, BMC or to Rootes Commer Karriers and Dodges. Leyland, Bedford and Fords produce the bulk of the heavier vehicles. The names of Seddon, Foden, ERF, Atkinsons, Guy, and Dennis are all well known for their quality vehicles demanded by the heavy haulage operators.

Vehicle weights

Within the transport industry there are a number of ways in which vehicles are referred to. Unless it is clear which term is being used there is almost bound to be confusion.

Those who use vehicles normally refer to a payload. Thus when a 7-ton lorry is mentioned this means a lorry with a weight carrying capacity of 7 tons. When a lorry is described officially by the Ministry of Transport or its Inspectors the reference is normally to the vehicle's unladen weight. This is the criterion for taxation purposes. More recently with the introduction of the new legislation one refers to "plated" weight. This is because under new legislation vehicles must bear on a plate on the vehicle chassis the total or gross weight allowable for the vehicle and its load. This is also known as gross vehicle weight or GVW.

Vehicles

The problems of weight distribution are aggravated by the requirement that the prescribed axle loading must not be exceeded. If a vehicle drops half a load on the way to its final destination it may be that the residual load will need to be handled into fresh positions to avoid overloading of an axle.

In addition, the comfort of the driver and the ergonomics of the driver's operation should also be taken into account. In delivery vehicles, for example, a driver may climb in and out of his cab something like two hundred times a day. This of itself can be a considerable physical strain if the cab steps are too high.

Engines

The engine accounts for about a quarter of the cost of a vehicle and its life is therefore of importance to the economics of operation. Diesel engines are usually used for heavy lorries and although they have been enjoyed for many decades now it would seem that they may be made still more efficient.

Most diesel engines in heavy lorries can be expected to run for about 250 000 miles (400 225 km) before a reconditioning and this may amount to a life of five years. Their high initial cost is insignificant when calculated in terms of miles run.

For light vans, however, the smaller mileages usually run do not yet justify the greater initial cost of the diesel compared to the petrol engine even though the fuel cost is less. Add to this the unfamiliarity of many garages and drivers used to private cars and petrol engines with diesel engines and fuel injection, and the reluctance to change to diesels is emphasised.

As motorways are developed and with higher weights for vehicles more power is needed. Power may be measured in terms of brake horse power. Private cars often have about 100 b.h.p. a ton. Six b.h.p. a ton is reasonable for a lorry on a motorway and more is required on other roads. For enough acceleration to give a decent performance, between 10 and 20 b.h.p. a ton is needed. But provision of more power above a certain weight does not need just bigger engines, but different engines and satisfactory solutions do not yet appear to have been marketed. Supercharging may be the answer.

Gear boxes

A medium-sized vehicle needs about five gears. One will be very low and one higher than for most cars. With bigger lorries however a greater range of gears is required. This may be provided by two ratios in a "splitter" box so as to allow eight or ten different speeds.

But the crown wheel which gears on to a smaller pinion in the rear differential may need to be so large that instead a double reduction axle may be used. Thus is the importance of torque accentuated. This is the driving twist of the engine. As far as possible this needs to be steady over the range of speed in the selected gear. This allows the driver to keep the engine revolutions a minute at an optimum level.

Brakes

The statutory requirement is that brakes must have an efficiency of 50 per cent. Vehicles must also have another independent system installed with an efficiency of 25 per cent. These percentages refer to the braking effect on the wheels as a percentage of the weight of the vehicle.

It is now common for heavy lorries to have air brakes powering the wheel brakes at each axle separately so that if one of the dual air assistance systems fails the other still provides a degree of braking.

Where trailers are used the problem of jack-knifing arises. This happens when there is imbalance in the braking system and a slippery road surface. If the rear wheels of the tractor unit lock, the trailer tends to surge forward and the loose rear end of the trailer snaps round. The tractor and trailer snap together on the hinge of the tractor rear wheels. Jack-knifing risk is reduced by altering the balance of the brakes and making the braking action relate to the weight of the load being carried or by controlling the swing. There are some systems available which prevent brakes locking at all.

Tyres

Increasing attention is paid, and needs to be paid in modern vehicle operation, to the proper servicing of tyres. These may also be bought on discount terms by fleet owners. The companies supplying tyres are, as an aid to selling, more and more offering advice on the satisfactory employment of their product. Some companies even go so far as to claim increased mileage through the fitting of tyres with special treads. They are prepared to substantiate their claims. With new legislation it is important to make frequent and proper checks on tyre wear, especially on the inside of the tyre wall, and to see that vehicles are run with tyres properly inflated. Drivers can, of course, contribute much to the extension of the life of tyres. Both excessive braking and vehicle overloading and unequal loading are responsible for unnecessary wear. The type of operation also affects the life of tyres. It would be absurd to attempt to compare the distance obtained from the tyres of a vehicle operating at high speeds on motorways with one operating in low-density traffic areas at relatively slow speeds. Stopping and starting in towns causes more tyre wear than operating in the country areas, provided the road surfaces are good.

Summary of chapter

1   The advantages and the disadvantages of fleet ownership can be enjoyed without investment by hiring.
2   Capital is thereby left available for other investment or as working funds.
3   Advice is often offered on the appropriateness of vehicles and the solution of other problems but, bearing in mind that the prime objective of the hiring organisation is to

hire vehicles, the advice given cannot always be disinterested.

4   As part of the contract there may be provided a vehicle replacement service and maintenance and drivers.

5   Ownership of hire of a fleet makes possible purchase on advantageous terms of fuel, lubricants, tyres, and sometimes spare parts.

6   A drawback of hiring is that the vehicle users must pay a reasonable return on the capital invested by the hirers; this is not always offset by economies of large-scale operation or efficient management.

7   The service promised is not always provided. If drivers as well as vehicles are hired they do not always identify their interests with those of the hirer.

8   The terms of the contract are variable provided they are legally enforceable and within the scope of governmental financial regulations.

9   Charges are normally on a time basis plus a mileage charge and this means cost plus. This can lead to operating inefficiency.

10   It is preferable that incentives to efficiency are built into the hiring arrangement. This is possible when vehicles are run on a schedule of prices for work done.

11   In long-term contractual arrangements an escalation clause may be incorporated.

12   When choosing the vehicles to be bought or hired one must consider

  (a) The type of body and cab bearing in mind the load and the activities of the driver.

  (b) Whether the vehicle is to be articulated or rigid.

13   Vehicles are described by their payload or by their unladen weight or by their gross vehicle weight.

14   Engines cost about one-quarter of the total vehicle cost. Bigger vehicles use diesel fuel and smaller vans use petrol.

15   The need for greater power and the use of bigger lorries is causing design problems.

16   The transfer of power for the movement of heavier vehicles required more sophisticated gearing.

17   Unbalanced brakes may lead to jack-knifing of articulated vehicles. This risk may be reduced by altering the balance of the brakes and making the brakes react in relation to the weight of the load carried.

18   Tyres are expensive and must be maintained with care. It is an offence to own a vehicle with improperly inflated tyres or when they are worn out. Drivers can extend the life of tyres by careful driving.

Depots and stocks

Thought must be given to the correct use of depots: they can be an asset or a waste, depending upon the stage at which they are introduced, the areas they are required to serve, and the volume of work they do.

Depots may be advisable for one or more of the following reasons:

1   To save the high cost of transport in small consign-
     ments for long distances and to gain the benefit of
     carriage in bulk.
2   To make available local stocks which can be
     supplied quickly to customers making urgent
     requests for supply and thus improving service.
3   To reduce costs of delivery where more than one
     factory is supplying one particular area by amal-
     gamating the deliveries made.

Renting a depot saves investment. On the other hand, there is a growing tendency to use warehousing and delivery agents to supply a storage and distribution service. By integrating services for a number of customers and as a result of operating efficiency, agents can match an individual user's own service at a reduced cost.

When deciding upon the establishment of depots, the follow-ing points should be borne in mind.

Present storage capacity

Existing storage facilities must be taken into account. An increase in storage capacity at depots may leave factory accommodation unused. If more space is provided, however, there is a likelihood that it will be used. If more space is not made available, more economic use must be made of existing space.

Size of depot

Each depot should be big enough to accept full loads or at least substantial parts of a full load on a big road or rail trunking vehicle.

Depot economics

Each depot should also be of sufficient size to allow economical operation of the depot. For example, there will probably need to be at least a manager or a supervisor and some handling staff. The traffic throughput is therefore important. Whilst it is frequently true that the bigger the depot the more economic it is to operate, there obviously comes a point where sheer size leads to inefficiency. Enormous depots handling a wide range of products are difficult to manage, but with modern handling and management techniques there are few instances in this country where a well-organised firm finds size an inhibition.

Much more often it is severe shortage of space which leads to inefficiency. But movements within the warehouse do get longer and organisation does get more complicated. As the depot grows, so does the need for more staff welfare amenities. Even allowing for this, the economies of size are usually very substantial indeed if full use is made of the capacity.

Delivery radius

The delivery radius must be economic. This tends to keep the number of depots up and the size of the depots down. Not only is it true that the delivery service provided when the delivery vehicle leaves the depot in the morning and returns at night is often more convenient, but also a limited delivery radius makes it easier for emergency deliveries to be made. If the depot is within easy reach of customers then, at times of emergency and maximum business, a customer may himself call and collect.

The actual area to be covered by the vehicles from one depot may be evaluated by trial and error. If on initial inspection a radius of 30 miles (48 km) seems appropriate then the effect of increasing the distribution radius to 40 (64 km) should be tested. Thereafter, the effect of reducing the area to 20 miles (32 km) should be tested.

Mathematical models are of considerable use in such situations. It must be remembered again, however, that the variations in transport operations are so great that realistic inspection and knowledge of operations are an indispensable check before acceptance of the result for action by management.

Geographical siting

As staff must be available to man the depots, these are most likely to be established near small towns. Location near big towns usually involves paying high rent. Recruiting drivers and warehouse men where there is a considerable amount of alternative employment available becomes expensive, yet, on the other hand, access to Freightliner terminals or motorways will have advantages, which can be easily seen on the maps (Figures 7:1–3.) If one centralised depot is desired then it is clear from the motorway map that this should be located in the area north of Birmingham and Coventry, if the inputs are by road. If the inputs are to be by rail, maximum accessibility is probably in the area north of London.

Because so often consumption of a firm's product is in areas of dense population, then it may be best to locate depots there. The map in Figure 7:3 illustrates these areas. (See Figure 7:3.)

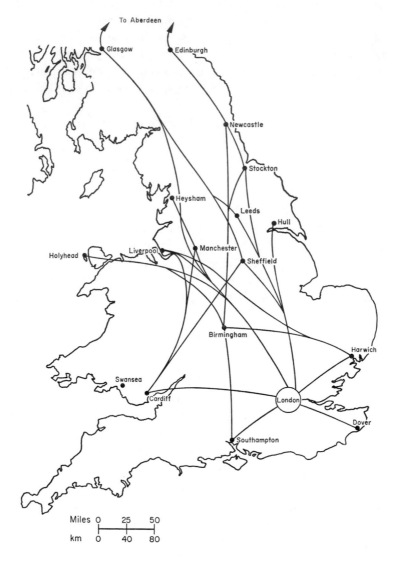

FIGURE 7:1   FREIGHTLINER ROUTES: PRINCIPAL SERVICES

FIGURE 7:2   MOTORWAYS AND TRUNK ROADS

Miles 0   25   50
km   0   40   80

FIGURE 7:3   CENTRES OF POPULATION AND PRODUCT DISTRIBUTION

Size of depot fleets

It will already have been observed that unit trunk costs, provided maximum use is made of the trunk vehicles, are low compared to overall distribution costs. Depot costs, provided they are efficiently manned and fully used, can also be low. The crucial consideration in most cases is the number of drops that can be effected by vehicles.

The number of delivery vehicles required is assessed in much the same way as a fleet requirement is assessed. The size and design of vehicles can affect the speed with which deliveries can be made where accessibility to a firm's premises is difficult. It is sometimes impossible to take big vehicles into crowded urban areas and it is often expensive to maintain big vehicles. Smaller vehicles are easier to look after and for smaller vehicles drivers may be tempted to undertake small repairs themselves. Drivers of small vehicles can sometimes be allowed to use them for private purposes and thus will be inclined to take greater care of their vehicles. Where occasionally large goods or large drops are involved it may be desirable not to gear the whole fleet to accommodate these but to have an occasional big vehicle available whilst the majority of the fleet is much smaller.

In some industries there is a tendency for manufacturers to group together to organise satisfactory distribution. This essentially necessitates formation of a separate company.

It may be true that a distribution system based on a large number of depots will produce operating costs lower than if deliveries are made direct from a factory or a central warehouse, but the return on the investment in the depot may be less than returns from investment possible elsewhere.

Capital allowances for storage depots

In a dispute concerning depot tax allowances between the Inland Revenue and Saxone, Lilley and Skinner (Holdings), which was eventually brought to the House of Lords in February 1967, judgement was given in favour of the company. It was established that the whole cost of a building but not the land on which the building stands can be treated as an expense for tax purposes if qualifying for the Industrial Buildings Allowance.

Now, if a warehouse is part of an industrial process, it qualifies for allowance, but if it is part of a retail distribution system, it does not. The relevant classification of industrial buildings requires "use" for the purpose of the trade and their storage of:

1   Goods and materials to be used in the manufacture of other goods or materials.
2   Goods or materials which are to be subjected, in the course of the trade, to any process.
3   Goods or materials which having been manufactured or produced or subjected to any process have not yet been delivered to any purchaser.
4   Goods or materials on their arrival by sea or air into any part of the UK.

In the Saxone, Lilley and Skinner (Holdings) Ltd case the company had a central depot at Leeds to store about half a million pairs of shoes received from various factories. From this depot shoes were distributed to shops throughout the country. A third of the shoes were manufactured by the company. This third was obviously "allowable" for tax purposes.

The Inland Revenue contended that because only a third, that is less than half the total, qualified for investment allowance then there should be no investment allowance at all. The House of Lords on appeal decided that one third was enough to satisfy the legal interpretation of the phrase "a part of a trade." It was not necessary for all the shoes or even half the shoes to be of Lilley and Skinner manufacture to qualify.

It was made clear however that where there were only intermittent or small proportions which qualified for allowances the same ruling could not apply.

The effect of this decision could materially affect the planning of a depot system. This is especially so if the depots being considered are in a development area.

Hired depot distribution services

Where the concentration of customers is below the level which makes it economic to distribute from own depots or in own vehicles there are normally two alternatives.

Local carriers

Goods can be handed over to a small carrier whose depot is located in the distribution area. The charge is normally calculated from the carrier's scales. It has been shown how the lower weight end of carrier's scales of charges are expensive per unit even though distances may be short. There is usually little to be gained by trunking and then offering the goods to a carrier who could do the trunking himself.

Distribution contractors

If for any reason trunking is better kept separate from distribution, or if stocks are required in given areas then there is a case for using the services of a warehousing and distribution contractor. Such a contractor will normally offer other services such as stock keeping, sales advices and may undertake other paper work.

These contractors normally specialise in broad categories of goods and areas. They combine deliveries in the same area from several manufacturers and in this way achieve operating efficiencies denied manufacturers operating on their own.

The storage space rented from a distribution contractor can be adjusted seasonally. Equally, the customer of a contractor only pays for the handling incurred in moving his goods, which must be compared to the cost of completely staffing a depot. If the specialist is efficient and uses adequate and suitable mechanical equipment, this higher utilisation of equipment can also reduce unit costs substantially over a long period.

Assuming storage costs of about 7d (3p) a square foot (929 cm²) a week, then the charges of a specialist distributor of about £8 a ton would include:

1	Receiving and dispatching products.
2	Storing for a period of three to four weeks.
3	Distribution over an area with a radius of about 40 to 50 miles (64–80 km).
4	Keeping records of stock, providing daily information of deliveries against orders passed in and some elementary statistics.

Depot expansion and investment

In a growing enterprise with expanding output there is a point at which it is necessary to expand the storage capacity. In the context of the company's growth, finance is probably being competed for keenly. At what stage of output does one acquire new facilities? Expansion adjacent to the manufacturing unit may be possible, but this is not often so where a firm has been established for some time and is in a built-up area.

One solution is to purchase or lease a central warehouse away from the manufacturing unit. This will involve extra movement from the manufacturing unit or units and handling but, as this will be in bulk, unit costs will be relatively low. Of particular interest is the stage in the programmed expansion at which the investment should be made. This is best determined by using the DCF technique.

Assuming that to accommodate the extra output before the investment is made storage space is hired from warehousemen. Then, ignoring the transport operation to and from these depots, the cost of storage will be known. If this is plotted on a graph the optimum point for changeover is demonstrable. This may be illustrated as is shown in Figures 7:4 and 7:5.

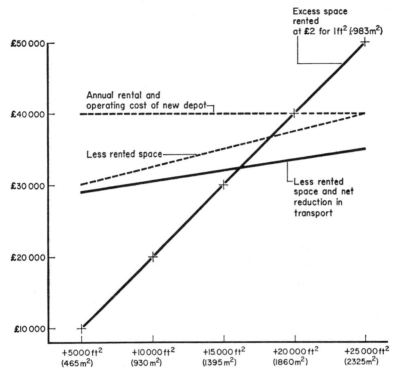

FIGURE 7:4 WHEN TO PURCHASE A CENTRAL OR BIGGER DEPOT

A firm which is expanding and diversifying rapidly in a number of factories has to decide at which point to move output into a central depot. The present need for extra space is met by renting storage areas in various warehouses at an average cost of £2 for each 1 ft² (929 cm²). Existing available area within the factory is 50 000 ft² (4645 m²).

A suitably placed warehouse becomes available at a rental of £30 000 a year and would provide a floor space of 250 000 ft² (6503 m²). Allowing for the movement necessary into the depot the central distribution makes a net saving in transport possible by better distribution planning of about £1000 for every 2500 tons throughput. This is the annual tonnage throughput each 5000 ft² (464.5 m²). The cost of operating the depot is £10 000.

111

Excess space in the new depot could be rented out at an average price of £1 for each 1 ft² (0.093 m²).

The situation may be illustrated graphically as is shown in Figure 7:4. When the extra space needed is over 16 250 ft² (15 096 m²) it becomes progressively more worth while to have the new depot.

Multi-factory supply to depots

Whilst the size of depots, in most cases, will be determined by the area served and the throughput, the problem may be to calculate the supply from a number of factories to particular depots. One way of solving this problem is to adopt a simple form of linear programming.

Assume supply points X, Y, and Z being three factories producing 1000 tons, 800 tons and 200 tons a period. The requirements of three depots A, B, and C are 700 tons, 800 tons and 500 tons respectively each period. The transport costs for each ton from supply points to the depots are as follows:

DEPOTS' UNIT SUPPLY COSTS

SUPPLY POINTS	A	B	C
X	£1	£1-5 (£1.25)	£1-10 (£1.50)
Y	£1-5 (£1.25)	15s (£0.75)	£1-5 (£1.25)
Z	£1-10 (£1.50)	£1	£1

Fill in from the top left corner:

	A (700 tons)	B (800 tons)	C (500 tons)
X (1000 tons)	700	300	
Y (800 tons)		500	300
Z (200 tons)			200

and the cost of this arrangement:

			£
$X - A$:	700 × £1		700
$X - B$:	300 × £1-5 (£1.25)		375
$Y - B$:	500 × 15s (£0.75)		375
$Y - C$:	300 × £1-5 (£1.25)		375
$Z - C$:	200 × £1		200
			£2025

112

It may not be the arrangement which minimises costs so adjust by loading other possibilities. This merely meant adding one unit and taking away to calculate the results.

	A		B		C
X	-1	699	$+1$	301	
Y	$+1$	1	-1	499	300
Z					200

Adjustment one: $-£1 + £1\text{-}5\,(£1.25) + £1\text{-}5\,(£1.25) - 15s$
$(£0.75) = +15s\,(£0.75)$
therefore this is no improvement and the adjustment increases cost.

Other adjustments are made by inspection and cost calculated and weighted according to the traffic moved until the optimum solution is reached, that is:

	A (700 tons)	B (800 tons)	C (500 tons)
X (1000 tons)	700		300
Y (800 tons)		800	
Z (200 tons)			200

and the cost of this arrangement:

		£
X — A:	700 × £1	700
X — C:	300 × £1-10 (£1.50)	450
Y — B:	800 × 15s (£0.75)	600
Z — C:	200 × £1	200
		£1950

Clearly in practice the situation may be complicated by existence of non-homogeneous products and supply of different goods from different factories. The method however is clearly adaptable to much more complicated situations.

113

Faster transit/lower stocks

The amount of stocks to be held will be determined by the sales and production managers rather than by the transport manager. Nevertheless, the transport manager will be asked on occasion to quantify the way in which expenditure on faster trunking or a faster service to the customer will affect the amount of stocks to be held. Assume a normal stockholding of £1 million, and a present service from the end of the production line into the main warehouse, from the main warehouse to depots and from the depots to customer of three weeks. If this could be reduced by better issuing disciplines and more rapid transport to two weeks the effect would be, at an expected rate of a return of 10 per cent on investment:

$$\frac{£1\,000\,000 \times 10\%}{50 \text{ weeks}} \times \frac{1}{3} = £666 \text{ saving/week}$$

Thus the cost of holding an extra week's stocks could be eliminated and the £666 a week saved may justify the cost of more sophisticated operation or more expensive transport. This is one of the significant items in the concept of "total distribution cost" a term of some popularity indicative of a new appreciation of what has been recognised in transport theory for a long time. What may be of more importance is that the financial liquidity of the company has probably improved.

Summary of chapter

1   Depots can be an asset or a waste depending on the stage at which they are introduced, the areas they are required to serve and the volume of work they do.

2   Depots can save the high cost of transport in small consignments for long distances, make available local stocks and make possible the amalgamation of deliveries.

3   Existing storage should not be duplicated.

4   Each depot should be big enough to accept full loads or

substantial part loads and big enough to allow economic operation.

5   The delivery service, which is usually a morning to evening trip operation, can only be within a limited area and thus keeps the number of depots up at the expense of the economics of size.

6   The actual area is best evaluated by trial and error first with mathematical models and then by inspection and with knowledge.

7   Depots are usually best located near towns and with access from the Freightliner terminals and motorways.

8   The size of the fleet and size and design of vehicles is assessed from the number of drops for each vehicle a day that can be effected and the nature of the goods.

9   Lower operating costs may be achieved through depots than direct from factories but the return on the investment in the depots may be less than returns possible from other investment.

10   Capital allowances for depots were tested in the case of Inland Revenue *v* Saxone, Lilley, and Skinner (Holdings) Limited in 1967.

11   If the customer concentration is too small in an area, either goods can be handed to carriers in specific areas or to distribution contractors who specialise in storage and delivery.

12   The exact point in a firm's business growth at which investment may be made in depots can be determined by mathematical simulation.

13   Linear programming can solve the problem of supply from a number of factories to a number of depots.

14   Stock-holding can be reduced by faster transits especially when supplying overseas customers.

EIGHT

Essential control information for transport management

Investment will have been decided upon by weighing the likely returns against the amount invested. Policy planning in transport is no different from that in other sections of an enterprise. It is equally necessary for the transport manager to be made aware of his level of efficiency. This awareness should not depend exclusively on a summons from the general manager after the firm has published its accounts. To be efficient the transport manager needs at least as rapid and continuous a supply of information as any other manager about how well he is doing or not doing.

It is usually believed that a major advantage in using a computer for the production of management information is that the computer can do the sums quickly. Whilst this is certainly so, thousands of sums, each of which would take about half an hour to complete by a clerk, being produced by a modern computer in a second, this very proficiency often leads to the concealing of relevant facts in a lot of irrelevant data. It is not uncommon for computer tabulations of great length to reach the desk of the transport manager, who, if he is to make a sensible allocation of his time to the problems of the day, has no choice but to sweep them into the waste-paper basket.

What the transport manager needs to help him to ensure

that there is no drift away from economic efficiency is a statement which:

1   Is brief enough for him to glance at.
2   Contains the information which highlights inefficiency.
3   Is produced quickly.

Statements that extend to more than one side of foolscap are probably too big. Statements which involve too much averaging are equally unsatisfactory. The nature of the compromise is critical.

Detailed explanations of faulty operations or of exceptional expenditure should be unnecessary. The transport manager can always ring up a depot manager or a colleague to find out what has happened.

There is sometimes a mistaken belief that statements produced for control purposes are always useful data for planning. This may or may not be so. The figures provided for long-term planning may need to be different from a daily or weekly statement produced to highlight an area of activity which the transport manager must investigate. The figures produced depend on what they are to be used for in each case. If transport planning is to be an integral part of the overall planning of a firm's activity, as it should, then the transport manager should be asked the questions. Reliance should not be placed on control data but on the answers to these questions.

Unit costs

Perhaps the quickest and simplest method of control is to calculate unit costs for activities. The unit costs can be by the ton, consignment, parcel, vehicle, load, sale, or anything else which is relevant.

For comparison between different types of activities they can be further computed per mile or per journey. The figures may be produced by the day, week, month, period, or year.

The commonest statistic of this character is the cost per ton mile. Where a number of operations are being compared the use of a ton mile is quite inappropriate. The cost per ton mile for a journey between London and Manchester with a full vehicle load will be very different to the cost per ton mile when undertaking distribution of small consignments in the West Country. Nevertheless, if these figures are compared day by day or period by period then violent fluctuations or adverse trends will highlight situations which require attention.

The most appropriate statistics for this general form of control are the cost per ton carried for trunk operations and the cost per drop for delivery operations. For different parts of the operation, there may be statistics of vehicle utilisation, use of drivers, and availability of equipment or productivity.

Comparisons with standards

These generalised figures often appear unreal when considering remedial action. Comparison of particular operations with standards is better, but the effort needed to produce sufficiently appropriate standards, and to keep them up to date, is great. One of the features of transport which proves attractive to managers, operators, and drivers is the variety of the work involved. This means that a lot of standard times have to be prepared before they can be synthesised with confidence. Nevertheless, the hard core of much transport conforms to certain patterns which repeat themselves. These patterns of operation must be examined and the methods used broken down and work-studied. The standards produced can then be set for regular operations or built into measurement for operations which vary from the normal.

If thereafter the usual common denominator of money is introduced as a base, actual performance can be measured against standard performance in monetary terms. This is often preferable to leaving the figures in the form of work study standards. Work efficiency, although important, is not necessarily the whole story when high value equipment, such as a modern lorry or modern handling plant, is involved.

Budgets

Modern sizeable firms and also most of those that are small need to control their flows of cash and their efficiency by budgeting ahead. A budget is normally prepared for each coming financial year and may o rmay not be adjusted as the year's trading develops. Sales are forecast with pricing policy and product promotions in mind. Estimates of expenditure are based on likely production, changed practice and unit costs.

The transport budget is estimated on the likely changes in costs, the growth or diminution of the services required and any changes in the character of the required service. It is usually based initially on the previous year's expenditures and modified in accordance with the firm's future policy and the knowledge available of changes in costs. Phasing of the budget is important. The annual forecast of revenue and expenditure can be divided into monthly or weekly or four-weekly periods. If these divisions are inappropriate they produce discrepancies or a "variance" which results in unreal comparisons. Adjustments are not always made for the fluctuating incidence of annual holidays, seasonal stockpiling or non-recurrent sales promotions. These must be taken into account.

Use of budgets for control is valuable. What is surprising is that budgets are frequently produced at a time when few of the managers involved have the time to sit back and think what will happen in the next twelve months. This would not be so bad if, during the twelve months for which the budget is made, so many boards of directors did not regard substantial variation from the forecast as failure. This seems to be so whether the income or expenditure is above or below the budget forecast. On the other hand, the variation may result from so many causes that failure to anticipate them may not always be culpable. Excessive sales, for example, may easily result in gross overspending on transport. Reduced sales may also lead to

119

greater spending on transport moving goods to store and involve the cost of storage when production is not reduced in time.

Where a company is part of a group, cash flow problems are multiplied and, without accurate estimation of cash requirements from the budget, a group can run into serious financial difficulty and substantial extra cost. It is important for adequate time to be given to the complications of the budget forecast. It is important for the plans of other departments to be taken into consideration at a time when the transport budget is compiled. Because questions are asked months later, it is worth keeping formal notes as to why the estimates are as they are. The opportunity should be taken, when forecasting for a budget, to review the success or lack of success of the previous year's plans and forecast. For most busy managers an occasional moment to sit back and review what has happened and to guess what is to happen is valuable in itself.

Excessive variation may result from inefficiency and this might have been avoided by different planning.

Hypothetical profit and loss

The danger in merely using budgetary measures and unit measures for control lies in the acceptance of, or at least the temptation to accept, previous and present transport costs as reasonable. Most conscientious transport men struggle constantly to keep down costs. The nature of the day-to-day management in which they are involved nevertheless sometimes tempts them to avoid rearrangements which disturb existing operations, especially if these operations have proved satisfactory. Where such disturbances result only in marginal benefits it may be wise to make no changes. But the services provided by carriers these days are changing so rapidly and the opportunities for use of one's own vehicles and of specialised equipment may be so great that the only satisfactory way to decide whether particular services are worth while is to prepare profit and loss statements for transport.

Some large organisations have the advantage of having isolated their transport activities by forming a separate transport company to supply the services they need either by themselves or by sub-contract. Others work together in association and are debited with "charges" from a non-profit-making organisation which is organised jointly. For others this is not always possible.

It is not easy, for example, to associate with keen competitors even though this might bring material advantages to all parties concerned. There is always the problem of providing preferential service to favoured customers; also the problem of control of an association by the members; not to mention the problem of the possible abuse of the overall advantage to the special advantage of some.

It is possible to assess the overall costs of transport whether in one's own or carriers' vehicles. It is less easy to assess the benefits of service, especially those which result from raising the standards of service. When running one's own vehicles a list of charges can be produced comparable to that of a carrier. An estimate can then be made of the "revenue" to transport. To this must be added the value placed upon the characteristics of service, such as emergency delivery and order taking.

The evaluation may be imprecise but is worth doing from time to time. Not only does it help to clarify the part to be played by the transport manager in the successful conduct of the business but it helps the other managers to understand the cost of their demands.

It is unnecessary to do such an evaluation continuously unless the accounting system is geared in such a way that the required figures are shown easily as the consequence of mechanisation or computerisation. Sample balance sheets for representative periods would be adequate. The periods for sample must be varied and must take into account fluctuation of business in the trading year. For example, it would be unwise always to assess the situation in the pre-Christmas peak or at a time of full production. It is necessary to take into account the off-peak and more normal working periods.

If a substantial loss is shown to be recurrent, the general management is put into a position where it can decide whether or not the service is worth while. It may be then decided whether it is worth while paying for the privilege of using one's own vehicles. The transport manager himself can see whether his contribution to the success of the business is either positive or negative.

Comparisons with alternatives

As mentioned in Chapter 6, the criterion as to whether one should provide one's own transport, use the services of others or contract for the provision of services by one carrier is the cost and the evaluation of the difference in the nature of the service provided. A difficulty is to establish the costs of using public carriers when the carriers know that the firm is geared to long-term private operation. Once, or possibly twice, a carrier will offer to study the services required and to offer a comprehensive deal for the provision of those services, but repetitive requests for such studies will only lead to either refusal or an offer to carry at published charges.

Firms of transport advisers exist which represent a large number of users of transport and, among other things, negotiate charges for transport. Such firms would be unlikely to recommend a service that would in the end prove unsatisfactory either to the user or to the provider. They could be employed to advise on the best carriers to use or to suggest alternatives. They might well be used to provide continuous advice of this kind as a check on whether movement in own vehicles could be bettered.

Summary of chapter

1   The transport manager needs at least as rapid and continuous a supply of information as any other manager about how well he is doing or not doing.

2   This information should be brief, contain the information which highlights inefficiency and is produced quickly. A statement covering more than one side of foolscap paper is probably too big.

3   Detailed explanations in the statement are undesirable. If he wants to know the reason for an unsatisfactory figure the transport manager can always ring up and find out.

4   Control statistics may be inappropriate for planning purposes.

5   Unit costs are dangerous if used as absolutes but their fluctuations in a series often provide useful pointers.

6   Comparison with standards provided by work study and measurement and synthetics are useful but the effort required to keep the standards up to date is considerable.

7   A transport budget is estimated on the likely changes in costs, the growth or diminution of the services required and any changes in the character of the required service.

8   Budgets should be produced when there is time to think about the future. Adjustment is preferable if prospects or circumstances change but as one of the reasons for preparing a budget is to estimate the cost flow requirements of the business this may not always be possible. An occasional guess forward has many advantages.

9   The danger in using budgetary and unit measures is that it tempts the transport manager to accept previous and present transport costs as reasonable. They may not be.

10   Some large organisations avoid this danger by setting up their own companies to compete with other carriers for their business.

11   Some join associations.

12   It is worthwhile producing a "profit and loss" account for a privately owned fleet from time to time.

13   This may be inexact but it will indicate to the transport manager how successful his teams' work is; it will also help illustrate to others the cost of their demands and

will clarify the contribution made by the transport organisation to the firm's net results.

14   The competition between one's own fleet and professional carriers may not be "fair." Professional carriers will be reluctant to spend their time studying a transport situation and making a competitive offer for the business if there is little chance of their obtaining it.

15   Transport advisers may be retained to advise as to what charges are currently available in situations which may arise and which carriers to choose or avoid.

NINE

The law and company transport

Attempts to achieve greater economic efficiency must, of course, be within the framework of safety and statutory obligations. Appreciation of the law and of technical requirements imposed on the operators of road vehicles is indispensable to successful operations. Requirements are precise. Requirements relevant to particular types of operation in particular industries need to be studied in detail. From the point of view of management an understanding is necessary of the range of obligations imposed. It is for this reason that the following comments are incorporated.

The conditions for operation of goods vehicles are determined by the principles of common law. This has been interpreted by numerous Acts, orders, and regulations. Whilst special study of the law of carriage would provide an interesting background for the conduct of a transport business, detailed study of such important acts even as the Carriers Act of 1830 is today rather more academic than practical. Detailed interpretation of the various regulations and statutory obligations is best left to the lawyers. Many of the obligations are in any case accepted as good practice by responsible operators. Transport and trade associations have played an important part not only in informing their members of the ramifications of requirements but in clarifying with the Ministry of Transport the problems which arise as the result of new legislation as it is proposed. The recommendations of trade associations often become part of the legislation.

The "rules" may be divided into four sections: driving carriers, vehicles, and insurance.

Driving

This is largely covered by the Road Traffic Act of 1960 and subsequent regulations. The offences which may be committed are:

1   Causing death by reckless or dangerous driving.
2   Driving in a manner or a speed which in the circumstances is dangerous to the public.
3   Driving without due care or attention or without reasonable consideration for other persons.
4   Exceeding any statutory speed limits.
5   Driving or permitting a person to drive when under age.
6   Driving or being in charge of a motor vehicle when under the influence of drink or drugs.

Speed limits apply to both roads and to vehicles. Where these differ the lower of the two limits applies. At the moment the maximum speed allowed is 70 miles an hour (112 km/h) for vehicles. Various roads are restricted to 50, 40, and 30 miles an hour (80, 64, 48 km/h). Other speed limits are shown on appropriate traffic signs. All goods vehicles are restricted on roads other than motorways to a maximum speed of 40 miles an hour (64 km/h). Goods vehicles towing trailers are restricted to a maximum speed of 30 miles an hour. Vehicles capable of carrying heavy loads or special loads are restricted to lower speeds. On motorways, goods vehicles are permitted to travel up to a speed of 70 miles an hour (112 km/h) unless they are hauling four-wheeled or special two-wheeled trailers. For these the limit is 40 miles an hour (64 km/h). On motorways goods vehicles are not allowed to use the third lane, normally known as the "overtaking lane," except when passing an abnormally wide load.

126

Where vehicles haul a trailer, which is not a part of an articulated unit, an extra person is required for driving or attending the vehicle.

A driver of a light van must be at least seventeen years old and before being allowed to drive a heavy lorry he must be twenty-one years old. The driver must hold a licence allowing him to drive that class of vehicle. Licences are granted upon passing a statutory test of competence to drive.

Wages to be paid to road haulage workers engaged by public carriers are fixed by the Road Haulage Wages Council and are set down in Wages Regulation Orders. Certain other provisions are also made in these Orders. Whilst these Orders do not apply to the operation of private fleets they do tend to establish a minimum for remuneration. A much more effective check on wages is, of course, the ability to attract suitable drivers and to retain them in the services of the company. Most drivers on trunk runs at the moment require the earnings equivalent of ten or eleven hours work a day for six days a week. They may not in fact drive or work for this time but to retain them it is necessary to pay such wages. As new legislation is introduced and drivers' permitted hours of work are reduced this is likely to lead to a demand to maintain existing income in return for the reduced work done. Bearing in mind the time many drivers spend on the job compared to their fellows doing shift work in factories this seems not only inevitable but also reasonably fair. Drivers undertaking a local distribution, however, are more inclined to accept the wages which allow them maximum return for lesser time spent on the job.

The driver will not be convicted for working hours greater than allowed by law if he can prove that the delay in completing his journey was due to circumstances beyond his control and which he could not have foreseen. These delays must of course be recorded immediately to prevent possible misunderstanding.

Importance of the correct keeping of drivers' records cannot be over emphasised. Regulations about hours of work records are specific. Records must show the hours of work completed, the journey, and the loads carried. These details must be entered on a record sheet by the driver as they become available and as work is completed. Very often it is convenient for a driver to complete the record at the end of a day's work. This is not permissible, for it must be done immediately. The driver must sign the completed form on the day the record is made and must return the form to his employer within seven days. There are four separate kinds of records or log sheets. They are more properly known as the "Daily records of hours worked, journeys, and loads." Their layout is specified in Government regulations. They are:

1   Drivers collecting and/or delivering within a radius of twenty-five miles.
2   Part-time drivers doing the same.
3   Full-time drivers on journey work.
4   Part-time drivers on journey work.

No-one is permitted to drive a goods vehicle:

1   For any period of more than five and a half hours continuously without a break of at least half an hour for rest and refreshment.
2   For more than a total of eleven hours in a period of twenty-four hours commencing at 02 00.
3   Unless the driver has at least ten consecutive hours of rest in any period of twenty-four hours calculated from the commencement of any period of driving.

It is permitted, however, that the driver may have nine hours' rest if he has twelve hours of rest during the next twenty-four hour period. In this context driving is considered to be time spent:

1   At the wheel.
2   Unloading and loading.
3   Completing documents, cleaning the vehicle, refuelling or checking tyres, batteries etc.

The hours of rest must not include any time when the driver has to follow the directions of his employer and remain on or near the vehicle. Rest can only be taken where reasonable facilities exist for proper rest. On the other hand, the half hour rest break may be taken on the vehicle if the driver has refreshment with him.

If two drivers are provided, by taking turns a driving schedule of fourteen hours may be maintained provided they take refreshment with them. Neither driver, of course, must exceed the five and a half hours driving spell or the eleven hour total. The ten hour rest period must also be allowed in any twenty-four hours. The costs of providing two drivers make this an uncommon practice for the regular movement of general goods in this country.

Where a statutory attendant is carried on a vehicle the hours of work he does should also be entered. There is no need for the attendant to sign the log sheet. If two drivers are engaged on the same vehicle, however, both must sign the log sheet.

The importance of the maintenance of proper records and the fact that this must be done is emphasised by the fact that Ministry of Transport certifying officers or uniformed police officers can and do inspect drivers' records at the road side. Both these groups of officers are permitted to hold a vehicle for as long as is necessary to examine or to copy information.

The only exception to all these stringent provisions is that the hours of work need not be recorded by a driver of a *C* licensed vehicle not exceeding 15 hundredweight (762 kg) unladen weight on a journey within 5 miles (8 km) of its base.

The log sheets must be kept for three months from the date the record is made. During this time they must be available for inspection by a Ministry of Transport examiner. If an inspection is made, it may be necessary to retain the forms for a period over three months but not more than six months.

The drivers' log sheets often provide useful information of vehicle journeys for analysis or when attempting improved routeing. In many ways they are a useful management control, too. It must be remembered, however, that drivers have been known sometimes to misrepresent their activities. However undesirable it may be and despite its illegality, it has been known for drivers to make a journey of many hundreds of miles without a rest period and for this not to be shown or to be shown as having taken considerably longer on the log sheet. Where such discrepancies are established it is wise to take effective action to prevent their recurrence. Anxiety to take one's wife out to the local hostelry for a leisurely pint on a Friday night is understandable but if the lives of other road users are endangered by an anxiety to get back home in a given time then the practice must be stopped. The danger to human life is supplemented by danger to an expensive vehicle and a valuable load. If a driver's own good sense does not ensure he realises this, it is worth while introducing a deterrent of suitable character to make sure that proper regard is paid to such regulations.

Carriers

The sections 164–70 of the Road Traffic Act of 1960, which consolidated the Road and Rail Traffic Act of 1933 and two Road Traffic Acts of 1934 and 1956, oblige users of goods vehicles whether for hire or reward or in connection with one's own trade or business to hold a carrier's licence issued by the appropriate licensing authority. There are eleven authorities with the following traffic areas: the Metropolitan, Northern, Yorkshire, North Western, West Midlands, East Midlands, Eastern, South Wales, Western, South Western, and Scottish.

There are three types of carriers' licences: A, public carriers' licence; B, limited carriers' licence; C, private carriers' licence.

A and B licences may have objections raised to their issue. Decisions are taken by the licensing authority after listening to the evidence. The C licence is normally granted on request by the licensing authority. Licences may not be transferred. A holding company can apply for licences for vehicles to be operated by a subsidiary company named in the application.

Vehicles

Control of vehicles is largely covered by the regulations known as Motor Vehicles (Construction and Use) Regulations 1966. These regulations are detailed and comprehensive and few operators need to know all the implications. Many of the regulations are of more direct interest to manufacturers of vehicles. Managers must be aware, on the other hand, of the general character of these regulations and must know to which of them they must pay particular attention from the point of view of their own business. The following definitions are of interest.

A *motor vehicle* is a mechanically propelled vehicle intended or adapted for use on roads. A *trailer* is a vehicle drawn by a motor vehicle. A *goods vehicle* is a vehicle constructed or adapted for the carriage of goods. This means that a trailer is a goods vehicle. Up to three tons weight unladen, vehicles are termed *motor cars*. Over this weight vehicles are termed *heavy motor cars*.

If the trailer is of such a nature that 20 per cent of its load, when uniformly distributed, is borne by the drawing vehicle, the tractor and trailer together are known as an *articulated vehicle*. For the purpose of issuing a licence an articulated vehicle is regarded as two units. For registration purposes it is regarded as one. Excise duty depends on the combined unladen weight of drawing vehicle and trailer.

A *motor tractor* is a vehicle not constructed to carry a load itself with an unladen weight not exceeding seven and a quarter tons. Over seven and a quarter tons "tractors" become *locomotives*.

The regulations provide for the maximum length and maximum width for vehicles. No maximum height is specified. Nevertheless excessive height can result in poor routeing because low bridges would have to be avoided. The maximum length for rigid motor vehicles is 36 feet 1 inch (10.99 m) for articulated vehicles 44 feet 7 inches (13.59 m) and for trailers 22 feet 11 inches (6.98 m). Maximum width for goods vehicles is 8 feet 2 inches (2.64 m) and this is the same for the bigger articulated trailers. For trailers, with certain exceptions, maximum width is 7½ feet (2.28 m). The maximum overhang permitted for goods vehicles is 60 per cent of the wheelbase. Standards are set for the efficiency of brakes and for the number of brakes on vehicles. There are also regulations for the fitting of speedometers, mirrors, safety glass, windscreen wipers, a horn, and silencers, etc. Vehicles must be so built as to avoid producing too much smoke or visible vapour or noise.

Vehicles must also be plated. A plate must be fitted to all vehicles built to the permissible maximum weight limit. This does not apply to vehicles restricted to the lowest weight limit in each category. Plates must show manufacturer's name, vehicle type, engine type, chassis or serial type, number of axles, maximum gross weight, and maximum tare weight. All new commercial vehicles over 30 hundredweight (1524 kg) unladen now have to be fitted with plates. Other vehicles will be plated on their first yearly test.

The permissible maximum loads for goods vehicles may be summarised as:

1   Rigid vehicles and trailers with two axles and a wheelbase of at least 12 ft (3.66 m)—16 tons.
2   If the vehicle is articulated and has three axles and a wheelbase of at least 18 ft (5.48 m)—24 tons.
3   If articulated with four or more than four axles and a wheelbase of at least 38 ft (11.58 m)—32 tons.

The total laden weight of a vehicle and trailer which is not articulated must not exceed 24 tons or 32 tons if it is with power assisted brakes.

New regulations came into effect on 1 April 1968 in connection with tyres. Tyres have to be suitable for the use for which the vehicle or trailer is being put and matched with the types of tyres fitted on other wheels. The tyre must be properly inflated. The tyre must not have a break in its fabric or a cut in excess of

1 inch or 10 per cent of the section width of the tyre. A cut must not be deep enough to reach the body cords. A tyre must not have any lump or bulge caused by a partial failure of the structure. The tyre must not have any proportion of the ply or cord structure exposed. The tyre tread pattern must have a depth of at least 1 mm throughout at least three-quarters of the breadth of the tread and round the entire outer circumference of the tyre.

So rigorous are the demands on vehicle construction and so important are the implications of spot checks on the road and at premises together with the annual tests, that a strict maintenance discipline is necessary. Whilst regular maintenance will be scheduled by engineers it is important that daily and weekly checks should be made on the fuel, oil and water, fan belt, brakes, steering, tyres, lights and reflectors, brake and light couplings systems, batteries, and the water cooling system.

Vehicles' excise licences must be obtained from the taxation department of the county council in whose area the vehicle is normally kept. Form RF4 is used and the completed form should be forwarded to the county council or county borough council (Motor Taxation Department) with:

1   The fee.
2   A valid certificate of insurance.
3   A supplier's invoice.
4   A weight certificate.

Licences may be renewed either at the County Taxation Office or at the local post office, provided that the licence is for the same duration as the previous one, that the old licence disc is produced and any change of ownership or address has been recorded in the registration book of the council, that no alteration is to be made to the vehicle for its use and that the application is made not more than fourteen days before the licence becomes effective and not more than fourteen days after the previous one has expired. When a vehicle is registered, a registration book is issued. This book should be signed by the owner and kept.

The taxation rate for commercial vehicles depends on use, construction, and unladen weight. Excise duty is heavy and there is constant complaint about this duty which, together with the tax on fuel, makes a very sizeable contribution to the Exchequer's income. When the number of miles travelled by larger commercial vehicles is considered, however, in a year the cost of the excise licence per mile run or per ton mile is seen to be modest.

Insurance

All vehicles on the road must be insured in accordance with the Road Traffic Acts. The owner and driver must effect insurance to cover liability in respect of compensation for injury caused to a third party and the cost of any emergency treatment resulting from an accident. A "third party" insurance normally covers not only this but also liability for damage to property. The indemnity provided is usually limited to £50 000 for any one accident. Most operators think it wise to take out a comprehensive policy which also includes fire and theft risks and includes costs of repairs to a vehicle following accidental damage. Most policies exclude liability to passengers should a passenger on a goods vehicle be injured in an accident.

Goods in transit

If greater insurance cover is required for goods being carried than that offered under the conditions of carriage stated by a carrier, then insurance can be bought through brokers or from insurance companies. Many insurers who offer to take the additional risk, however, require vehicles to be fitted with anti-theft devices. They normally also insist that when vehicles are left overnight with their loads, they must not be left unattended unless immobilised, locked, and left in a building or yard which is also securely closed and locked. Such premises are often also guarded by security officials and guard dogs.

Summary of chapter

1 The conditions for the operation of goods vehicles are determined by the principles of common law interpreted by Acts, orders and regulations. Driving is covered mainly by the Road Traffic Act 1960 and subsequent regulations.

2 The correct keeping of drivers' records of hours of work is important and may be checked by Ministry of Transport certifying officers or uniformed police. These records must be kept for at least three months.

3 Driving offences are largely covered by the Road Traffic Act of 1960 and subsequent regulations.

4 To carry goods a carrier's licence must be obtained (in future it will be an operator's licence).

5 Operational control of vehicles is covered by the Motor Vehicles (Construction and Use) Regulations 1966. These among other things provide for maximum dimensions, standards of braking efficiency, provision of safety equipment and "plating," to show maximum permissible gross weight of vehicle and load.

6 Excise duty depends on use, construction and unladen weight of vehicles.

7 Vehicles must be insured for at least third-party risks but it is wiser to cover for other liabilities as well.

TEN

The future and the 1968 act

The Transport Act 1968 provides for the establishment of a National Freight Corporation and prescribes its duties and sets out financial provisions. To this corporation is transferred responsibilities for the following organisations:

1   British Road Services and BRS Contracts, and the Transport Holding general hauliers, of which there are many.
2   Pickfords Limited and Pickfords Heavy Transport, the Containerway and Road Ferry services and British Rail's Ferry services and others on short sea crossing routes.
3   Pickfords Tank Services and other tank vehicle operators such as Harold Wood and Sons and the Caledonian Bulk Liquid Company, and so on.
4   British Rail's Sundries Division, BRS Parcels and other parcels carriers within the T H Company's organisations, such as Bridges Transport, Tartan Arrow, Hansons, and so on.

The corporation will have a 51 per cent interest in the Freightliner Company (British Rail have a 49 per cent interest) and a 50 per cent interest, in this case shared with the Northern Ireland Government in Northern Ireland Carriers.

The Act brings about further changes in the law with important implications for transport managers.

New rules affecting carriage by road

Part V of the Act introduces new rules for the carriage of goods by road. The important changes will introduce a situation which may be outlined as follows:

1   No person may operate for hire or reward or for or in connection with any trade or business carried on by him except with an operator's (or carrier's) licence. This does not apply to the use of smaller vehicles up to a plated weight of $3\frac{1}{2}$ tons, that is the gross vehicle weight, or an unladen weight of 30 hundredweight (1.52 tonnes).

2   The licence must be granted in the area in which the vehicle has its operating base. This effectively terminates the past practice of bigger companies of licensing centrally.

3   New vehicles and vehicles no longer used or transferred to another licence must be notified to the licensing authority.

4   Full details of the intended use to which the vehicles will be put and various information about the applicant himself will be required.

5   Applications involving substantial increases in number of vehicles will be published.

6   The licencing authority must consider applications bearing in mind the following requirements:

    (a) That the applicant is a fit person, and this may involve consideration of available financial resources.

    (b) That there will be at each operating centre a person who is the holder of a transport manager's licence of the prescribed class and that the holder occupies a specified post.

(c) That the part of the Act dealing with drivers' hours shall be observed.

(d) That there will be satisfactory facilities for maintaining the vehicles and this in no way will be prejudiced by inadequate financial resources.

The responsibility for operation and maintenance of the authorised vehicles may be shared by two or more people provided they are specified in the licence and their particular responsibilities are also specified. Licences will normally be granted for five years.

The heavy responsibility firmly allocated to specific managers is emphasised by the possibility of fines of up to £200 and revocation of licences and in some circumstances imprisonment. Thus a transport manager's licence may be revoked, suspended, or curtailed, and with it may come loss of livelihood if:

1   A false statement was made or a statement of intention or expectation has not been fulfilled.

2   The holder has been adjudged bankrupt or has gone into liquidation (this not being voluntary liquidation for the purpose of reconstruction).

3   There has been a material change of relevant circumstances.

4   There has been a conviction for contravention of the requirement to

(a) Keep vehicles in fit condition.

(b) Observe speed limits, weight laden and unladen, and loading.

(c) Observe the conditions of the issue of the transport manager's licence.

(d) Observe prescribed driver's hours.

(e) Keep proper records.

(f) Infringe a sufficient number of times the regulations prohibiting or restricting the waiting of vehicles.

(g) Observe other statutory requirements.

138

Special authorisation for certain road traffics

Special authorisations must be obtained to carry in vehicles with a plated weight of over 16 tons or an unladen weight of over 5 tons if no plate, between places separated by a distance of more than 100 miles (161 km), even if in a container transferred to one or more other vehicles or if part of the journey is on a ferryship. These are miles as the crow flies. A special authorisation is also required for certain bulk traffic for distances of less than 100 miles (161 km) as well. The traffics considered to be bulk will probably be coal, coke and briquettes; extracted materials such as limestone flux and calcareous stone, clay and china clay and similar materials, dolomite, slag and iron and steel waste, iron ore and concentrates, but not roasted iron pyrites; iron and steel scrap, pig and cast iron, ingots and billets, blooms, and so on, and bars, rods, shapes and sections, plates, sheets, hoops, and strip iron and steel.

Objections to special authorisations may be lodged by the British Rail Board and the National Freight Corporation. If an objection is made then the objector must submit a statement of the way in which the services can be provided wholly or partly by rail and charges for the service. The applicant must in turn make a statement.

The judgement made by the licensing authorities will be on the grounds of speed, reliability, cost and other matters relevant to the needs of the person for whom the goods are to be carried.

Substantiation of a case for or against the granting of special authorisation is going to need the submission of a detailed cost data. The allocations of cost to particular traffics will have to be reasonable and justifiable. Just as was discussed in Chapter 3, if a rail service is considered unsatisfactory because of suspected unreliability, then the financial consequences to the customer of failure to deliver or of delay must be estimated. Cost in such circumstances will include those of holding stocks or the consequences of production shortfall or customer dissatisfaction. If the complaint is of damage, the

139

cost of insurance to indemnify, quantification of customer dissatisfaction, or the cost of extra packing might need to be tabled. Obviously support might be called in from a customer in the presentation of evidence. The Minister himself is empowered to define the scope of costs but this is not going to be an easy task. If refusal to grant a special authorisation would upset one leg of an operation which is between three or more points or affects a back load operation with a non bulk traffic for example, the consequence might seriously affect a fleet's economic operation. One might need to quantify the cost of sales service and customer contact by drivers for this might be a relevant and a permissible factor.

Difficult or not, realistic attempts to quantify the various factors involved will be required. The licensing authority will need facts. They will get facts from the NFC or British Rail. There is too much at stake for the Freightliner Company and the British Rail Board not to deploy a great deal of their best talent to select the cases most favourable to rail movement before venturing to object, and then to put in a lot of work making out the best possible case. Unless the applicant uses modern investment appraisal techniques such as described earlier and makes sensible allocations of cost and backs the arguments advanced with adequate data then the case for the applicant will be conducted from a position of disadvantage.

Where a traffic movement is urgent or which could not have been foreseen and an objection could not have succeeded, then a special authorisation may be granted by the licensing authority.

Various terms and conditions may be incorporated in the special authorisation. To help enforce this a consignment note showing carrier, destination, consignee and goods carried, must be completed, carried by the driver, and kept for a prescribed period.

Part VI of the Act deals with driver's hours. Driving time for this purpose is the time spent at the wheel of the vehicle with the engine running. Driving time must not exceed ten hours in a working day. The maximum time without a rest is five and a half hours. Thereafter a rest break of at least half an hour is necessary. The driving time of ten hours must not be spread over more than twelve and a half hours, it used to be fourteen, and the time on duty must not be more than eleven hours. Drivers' hours in a week must not exceed sixty hours and a driver must have a full twenty-four hours off duty in each working week. It is not certain when the reduction of drivers' hours will come into effect but that this might be but a step towards a further reduction.

No driver shall drive a vehicle unless there is installed equipment for recording information as to the use of the vehicle and this is in working order. Such tachograph records must be made available for inspection by police or inspectors' offices on request. Drivers have to keep records of their work.

In so far as the Act contributes to the safe operation of vehicles it must be applauded. That it pins down responsibilities for observation of sensible statutory requirements is also sound even though initially the acceptance of a professionalism will not be easy for the few transport managers who over the years have failed to prevent, for example, the over-loading of vehicles or drivers carrying on over the permitted hours.

Economic effects of the Act

The White Paper which preceded the Act, however, stated that a prime target was the elimination of wasteful competition and duplication within the publicly owned transport system. If such a policy increases efficiency and reduces cost then all will benefit. If, on the other hand, it establishes pockets of monopoly within the industry it could make the situation worse for the users of transport. Undoubtedly the restrictions on operation of bigger vehicles will aid the state owned organisations. It is the big lorries which if fully used keep down transport costs.

Such are the inevitable imprecisions of costing particular traffic movements by railway, where a major part of the costs stands for many years, that any charge which covers out of pocket expenses could be justified. It is unlikely that British Rail would take such an advantage more than marginally, but it could. If, for example, marginal costing and marginal pricing were introduced in the short run this might be a most sensible policy decision for a railway with a network of routes and assets now more or less fixed. In such a situation the need is to push as much traffic as possible through the system to keep unit costs low and so to remain competitive. But if after practising this policy for some years the railway's competitors were unable to continue to provide services and went out of business, it might be a temptation for railway prices to be raised again. Such a rise would allow a monopoly profit element to be secured. The rise could not be excessive of course because if it were a special authorisation would be sought and probably granted. It takes lower returns to keep an existing operator in business, however, than to bring in a new one. This is especially so if the risk of renewal of a competitive price cutting policy seems possible. This problem must not be exaggerated, of course, it only applies where the Freightliner Company or British Rail provide adequate services and compared to the total demand for services in this country this is for a relatively small tonnage of the total goods to be moved, especially if coal and steel are discounted. Any traffic transfer to rail will be made up in a few years by the growth of demand for transport in an expanding economy.

It will be a pity if the demarcation of 16 tons (16.15 t) gross vehicle weight introduces a criterion to vehicle designers which diverts their effort from the design of vehicles which can be operated with maximum technical and economic efficiency.

Freedom to carry other people's goods in C licence vehicles may not have the repercussions some public carriers fear. As has been mentioned, it is not always easy for firms in competition with one another to collaborate to mutual benefit in distribution. As it may be desirable to associate for transport when the product is of a like type this tends to limit the field for association. Where there exists the most promising opportunity for co-operation is where a firm employs its vehicles for only a limited period of the day and the vehicles would otherwise be standing idle. This may be true of the vehicles owned by newspaper proprietors. There is a belief that many private vehicles run empty for many miles back to their base, but this is seldom borne out by closer inspection except where it is economic to do so in order that the vehicle is available for the next prescribed outward load. Impartial investigations have in the past demonstrated that empty mileage run by C licence vehicles is not much more than that run by vehicles owned and operated by the professionals. Nevertheless there will be some occasions where a back load may be obtained which before the Act would have been refused.

To sum up, the trend is toward professionalism. In a sense therefore the Act crystallises many movements within the industry to this end. Unlike much previous transport legislation the Act is appropriate to current thinking. From the point of view of company freight transport this means either the employment of executives with an understanding of modern management techniques and up-to-date methods and the ability to ensure that statutory obligations are observed, or subcontracting transport planning and the carriage of goods to the professionals. This is not an easy choice and may be avoided by compromise. As transport managers will have to spend more time than ever to ensure effective controls then the planning may have to be put into the hands of those with the skill and resources to undertake such work. Transport managers themselves must not be considered missionaries even though much of their work must be to dispel the ignorance and prejudice which exists about their work. As they assume the responsibilities now to be imposed on them by statute, and the best have for long accepted these responsibilities anyway, so they will be able to require a satisfactory reward for the job they do. The financial risk of transport failure to most companies is too great for it to be otherwise.

Summary of chapter

1   The 1968 Transport Act has changed and will change the future framework in which company freight will be managed.

2   It has set up a massive state owned freight corporation for the movement of goods.

3   This corporation includes the Freightliner Company which will provide rail truck services for containers and a growing combination of road and rail services for small consignments.

4   Vehicles with a plated weight of up to $3\frac{1}{2}$ tons no longer need operators' licences to carry.

5   Vehicles with a plated weight of more than 16 tons carrying for more than 100 miles and those carrying bulk traffic will require special authorisation to operate.

6   Transport managers must also be licensed and will be responsible for the safe operation of the vehicles they control and that statutory obligations, such as the prescribed drivers' hours, are observed.

7   Transport managers must also have available adequate financial resources, for example, to ensure adequate vehicle maintenance is possible.

8   Objections to special authorisation may be by the British Rail Board or the NFC.

9   Objections will be heard by the licensing authority and considered on the grounds of service speed, reliability, cost, and other matters relevant to the needs of the person for whom the goods are to be carried.

10 Cases before the licensing authority for special authorisation will require the submission of detailed cost data and estimation of the financial consequences of aspects of service which are now rarely quantified.

11 The costs relevant to a particular operation will also require consideration. The Minister may define the scope of costs.

12   To provide relevant facts for the consideration of the Licensing Authority use should be made of modern management techniques.

13   The hours a driver can drive will, after an appointed day, be restricted to ten in a working day. To check this is observed there must be a tachograph on the vehicle and it must be in working older.

14   Freedom to carry other people's goods for hire and reward may change the operating patterns of privately owned vehicle fleets but because of the need to return to base quickly to ensure availability for the next load of a firm's own goods, this change may be less dramatic than some anticipate.

15   The Act emphasises the need for professionalism in the road transport industry and this is broadly in keeping with the spirit of the industry.

Conditions of carriage

The following *Conditions of carriage* are issued for the guidance and use of carriers; they are reproduced here by permission of the Road Haulage Association. (See *Discussion of claims* in Chapter 5.)

Conditions of carriage

Name and address of carrying company

The carrying company (hereinafter referred to as the "carrier") accepts goods for carriage subject to the conditions (hereinafter referred to as "these conditions") set out below. No agent or employee of the carrier is permitted to alter or vary these conditions in any way unless he is expressly authorised to do so.

1   Definitions

In these conditions the following expressions shall have the meanings hereby respectively assigned to them, that is to say:

Trader shall mean the customer who contracts for the services of the carrier.

Consignment shall mean goods in bulk or contained in one parcel or package, as the case may be, or any number of separate parcels or packages sent at one time in one load by or for the trader from one address to one address.

Dangerous goods shall mean:

146

(a) Goods which are specified in the special classification of dangerous goods issued by the British Rail Board or which, although not specified therein, are not acceptable to the British Rail Board for conveyance on the ground of their dangerous or hazardous nature.

(b) Goods which though not included in (a) above are of a kindred nature.

Contract shall mean the contract of carriage between the Trader and the Carrier.

Sub-contracting parties includes all persons (other than the Carrier and the Trader) referred to in clause 3(c).

Carrier save in the expression carrier/contractor includes sub-contracting parties in clauses 4(b), 5(b) and (c), and 11 (proviso).

Carrier/contractor means the Carrier and any other carrier within clause 3(2).

2   *Carrier is not a common carrier*

The carrier is not a common carrier and will accept goods for carriage only on these conditions.

3   *Parties and sub-contracting*

(a) Where the trader is not the owner of some or all of the goods in any consignment he shall be deemed for all purposes to be the agent of the owner or owners.

(b) The carrier may employ the services of any other carrier for the purpose of fulfilling the contract. Any such other carrier shall have the like power to sub-contract on like terms.

(c) The carrier enters into the contract for and on behalf of himself and his servants, agents, and sub-contractors and his sub-contractors' servants, agents, and sub-contractors; all of whom shall be entitled to the benefit of the contract and shall be under no liability whatsoever to the trader or anyone claiming through him in respect of the goods in addition to or separately from that of the carrier under the contract.

147

(*d*) The trader shall save harmless and keep the carrier indemnified against all claims or demands whatsoever by whomesoever made in excess of the liability of the carrier under these conditions.

4   *Dangerous goods*

(*a*) If the carrier agrees to accept dangerous goods for carriage such goods must be accompanied by a full declaration of their nature and contents and be properly and safely packed in accordance with any statutory regulations for the time being in force for transport by road.

(*b*) The trader shall indemnify the carrier against all loss, damage or injury however caused arising out of the carriage of any dangerous goods, whether declared as such or not.

5   *Loading and unloading*

(*a*) When collection or delivery takes place at the trader's premises the carrier/contractor shall not be under any obligation to provide any plant, power, or labour which, in addition to the carrier/contractor's carmen, is required for loading or unloading at such premises.

(*b*) Any assistance given by the carrier beyond the usual place of collection or delivery shall be at the sole risk of the trader, who will save harmless and keep the carrier indemnified against any claim or demand which could not have been made if such assistance had not been given.

(*c*) Goods requiring special appliances for unloading from the vehicle are accepted for carriage only on condition that the sender has duly ascertained from the consignee that such appliances are available at destination. Where the carrier/contractor is, without prior arrangement in writing with the Trader, called upon to load or unload such goods the carrier shall be under no liability whatsoever to the trader for any damage however caused, whether or not by the negligence of the carrier, and the trader shall save harmless and keep the carrier indemnified against any claim or demand which could not have been made if such assistance had not been given.

6   *Consignment notes*

The carrier/contractor shall, if so required, sign a document prepared by the sender acknowledging the receipt of the consignment; but no such document shall be evidence of the condition or of the correctness of the declared nature, quantity, or weight of the consignment at the time it is received by the carrier/contractor.

7   *Transit*

(*a*) Transit shall commence when the consignment is handed to the carrier/contractor whether at the point of collection or at the carrier/contractor's premises.

(*b*) Transit shall (unless otherwise previously determined) end when the consignment is tendered at the usual place of delivery at the consignee's address within the customary cartage hours of the district.

Provided:

i   That if no safe and adequate access or no adequate unloading facilities there exist then transit shall be deemed to end at the expiry of one clear day after notice in writing (or by telephone if so previously agreed in writing) of the arrival of the consignment at the carrier/contractor's premises has been sent to the consignee

ii That when for any other reason whatsoever, a consignment cannot be delivered or when a consignment is held by the carrier/contractor "to await order" or "to be kept till called for" or upon any like instructions and such instructions are not given, or the consignment is not called for and removed, within a reasonable time, then transit shall be deemed to end.

8   *Undelivered or unclaimed goods*

Where the carrier/contractor is unable for whatever reason to deliver a consignment to the consignee, or as he may order or where by virtue of the proviso to clause 7(*b*) hereof transit is deemed to be at an end the carrier/contractor may sell the goods and payment or tender of the proceeds after deductions of all proper charges and expenses in relation thereto and all outstanding charges in relation to the carriage and storage of the goods shall (without prejudice to any claim or right which the trader may have against the carrier otherwise arising under these conditions) discharge the carrier/contractor from all liability in respect of such goods, their carriage and storage.

Provided that:

(*a*) The carrier/contractor shall do what is reasonable to obtain the value of the consignment.

(*b*) The power of sale shall not be exercised where the name and address of the sender or of the consignee is known unless the carrier/contractor shall have done what is reasonable in the circumstances to give notice to the sender, or if the name and address of the sender is not known, to the consignee that the goods will be sold unless within the time specified in such notice, being a reasonable time in the circumstances from the giving of such notice, the goods are taken away or instructions are given for their disposal.

9   *Carrier's charges*

(*a*) The carrier's charges for carriage shall be payable by the trader without prejudice to the carrier's rights against the consignee or any other person. Provided that when goods are consigned "carriage forward," the trader shall not be required to pay such charges unless the consignee fails to pay after a reasonable demand has been made by the carrier/contractor for payment thereof.

(*b*) Except where the quotation states otherwise all quotations based on a tonnage rate shall apply to the gross weight, unless the goods exceed 80 cubic feet (2.3 m³) in measurement per ton weight, in which case the tonnage rate shall be computed upon and apply to each measurement of 80 cubic feet or any part thereof.

(*c*) A claim or counterclaim shall not be made the reason for deferring or withholding payment of monies payable, or liabilities incurred, to the carrier.

10   *Time limit for claims*

The Carrier shall not be liable:

(*a*) i For loss from a package or from an unpacked consignment; or

ii For damage, deviation, misdelivery, delay or detention; unless he is advised thereof in writing otherwise than upon a consignment note or delivery document within three days and the claim be made in writing within seven days after the termination of transit.

(*b*)   For loss or non-delivery of the whole of the consignment or of any separate package forming part of the consignment.

—unless he is advised of the loss or non-delivery in writing (other than upon a consignment note or delivery document) within twenty-eight days and the claim be made in writing within forty-two days after the commencement of transit.

11   *Liability for loss and damage*

Subject to these Conditions the Carrier shall be liable for any loss, or misdelivery of or damage to goods, occasioned during transit unless the carrier shall prove that such loss, misdelivery or damage has arisen from:

(*a*) Act of God.

(*b*) Any consequences of war, invasion, act of foreign enemy, hostilities (whether war be declared or not), civil war, rebellion, insurrection, military or usurped power or confiscation, requisition, destruction of, or damage to property by or under the order of any government or public or local authority.

(c) Seizure under legal process.

(d) Act or omission of the trader or owner of the goods or of the servants or agents of either.

(e) Inherent liability to wastage in bulk or weight, latent defect or inherent defect, vice or natural deterioration of the goods.

(f) Insufficient or improper packing.

(g) Insufficient or improper labelling or addressing.

(h) Riots, civil commotion, lockouts, general or partial stoppage or restraint of labour from whatever cause.

(j) Consignee not taking or accepting delivery within a reasonable time.

Provided that the carrier shall not incur liability of any kind in respect of a Consignment where there has been fraud on the part of the trader or the owner of the goods or the servants or agents of either in respect of that consignment.

12 *Limitation of liability*

Subject to these conditions the liability of the carrier in respect of any one consignment shall in any case be limited:

(a) Where the loss or damage however sustained is in respect of the whole of the consignment to a sum at the rate of £800 a ton on either the gross weight of the consignment as computed for the purpose of charges under clause 9 hereof or where no such computation has been made, the actual gross weight.

(b) Where loss or damage however sustained is in respect of part of a consignment to the proportion of the sum ascertained in accordance with (1) of this condition which the actual value of that part of the consignment bears to the actual value of the whole of the consignment. Provided that:

i Nothing in this clause shall limit the carrier's liability below the sum of £10 in respect of any one consignment.

ii The carrier shall not in any case be liable for indirect or consequential damages or for loss of a particular market whether held daily or at intervals.

iii The carrier shall be entitled to require proof of the value of the whole of the consignment.

13 *General lien*

The carrier shall have a general lien against the owner of any goods for any monies whatsoever due from such owner to the carrier. If any lien is not satisfied within a reasonable time the carrier may at his absolute discretion sell the goods as agents for the owner and apply the proceeds towards the monies due and the expenses of the sale, and shall upon accounting to the trader for the balance remaining, if any, be discharged from all liability whatsoever in respect of the goods.

14 *Unreasonable detention*

The trader shall be liable for the cost of unreasonable detention of vehicles, containers, and sheets but the carrier/contractor's rights against any other person shall remain unaffected.

15 *Computation of Time*

In the computation of time where the period provided by these conditions is seven days or less, the following days shall not be included:

In England and Wales: Sundays and Bank Holidays.
In Scotland: Sundays, and 1 January,
Spring and Autumn Holidays.

Extracts from the 1968 Transport Act

Arrangement of Sections

PART V

REGULATION OF CARRIAGE OF GOODS BY ROAD

The licensing authority

PART V

REGULATION OF CARRIAGE OF GOODS BY ROAD

The licensing authority

59—(1) In relation to each traffic area constituted for the purposes of
Part III of the Act of 1960, the person who is the chairman of the traffic
commissioners for the area (including any person for the time being

appointed by the Minister to act as deputy to the chairman) shall be known as the licensing authority and shall exercise the functions conferred on him by this Part of this Act and by Schedule 9 thereto.

(2) In the exercise of his functions under this Part of this Act and the said Schedule the licensing authority shall act under the general directions of the Minister.

(3) Each licensing authority shall make to the Minister an annual report of his proceedings, containing particulars with respect to such matters as the Minister may direct.

(4) Subsection (1) of this section shall have effect as respects the Metropolitan Traffic Area with the substitution of a reference to the traffic commissioner for the Metropolitan Traffic Area for the reference to the chairman of the traffic commissioners.

Operators' licences

60—(1) Subject to subsection (2) of this section and to the other provisions of this Part of this Act, no person shall, after the appointed day for the purposes of this section, use a goods vehicle on a road for the carriage of goods—

(*a*) for hire or reward; or

(*b*) for or in connection with any trade or business carried on by him, except under a licence granted under this Part of this Act (hereafter in this Part of this Act referred to as an "operator's licence").

(2) Subsection (1) of this section shall not apply—

(*a*) to the use of a small goods vehicle as defined in sub-section (4) of this section; or

(*b*) to the use of a vehicle of any class specified in regulations.

(3) It is hereby declared that, for the purposes of this Part of this Act, the performance by a local or public authority of their functions constitutes the carrying on of a business.

(4) For the purposes of subsection (2)(*a*) of this section a small goods vehicle is a goods vehicle which—

(*a*) does not form part of a vehicle combination and has a relevant plated weight not exceeding three and a half tons or (not having a relevant plated weight) has an unladen weight not exceeding thirty hundredweight; or

(*b*) forms part of a vehicle combination (not being an articulated combination) which is such that—

(i) if all the vehicles comprised in the combination (or all of them except any small trailer) have relevant plated weights, the aggregate of the relevant plated weights of the vehicles comprised in the combination (exclusive of any such trailer) does not exceed three and a half tons;

(ii) in any other case, the aggregate of the unladen weights of those vehicles (exclusive of any such trailer) does not exceed thirty hundredweight; or

(*c*) forms part of an articulated combination which is such that—

(i) if the trailer comprised in the combination has a relevant plated weight, the aggregate of the unladen weight of the motor vehicle comprised in the combination and the relevant plated weight of that trailer does not exceed three and a half tons;

   (ii) in any other case, the aggregate of the unladen weights of the motor vehicle and the trailer comprised in the combination does not exceed thirty hundredweight.

In any provision of this subsection "relevant plated weight" means a plated weight of the description specified in relation to that provision by regulations; and in paragraph (b) of this subsection "small trailer" means a trailer having an unladen weight not exceeding one ton.

   (5) A person who uses a vehicle in contravention of this section shall be liable on summary conviction to a fine not exceeding £200.

   61—(1) Subject to subsection (2) of this section, the vehicles authorised to be used under an operator's licence shall be—

   (a) such motor vehicles, being vehicles belonging to the holder of the licence or in his possession under an agreement for hire-purchase, hire or loan, as are specified in the licence;

   (b) trailers from time to time belonging to the holder of the licence or in his possession under an agreement for hire-purchase, hire or loan, not exceeding at any time such maximum number as is specified in the licence;

   (c) unless the licence does not permit the addition of authorised vehicles under this paragraph and subject to subsection (3) of this section, motor vehicles not exceeding such maximum number as is specified in the licence, being vehicles belonging to the holder of the licence or in his possession under an agreement for hire-purchase, hire or loan, but acquired by him, or coming into his possession under such an agreement, only after the grant of the licence.

For the purposes of paragraphs (b) and (c) of this subsection different types of trailers or different types of motor vehicles, as the case may be, may be distinguished in a licence and a maximum number may be specified in the licence for trailers or vehicles of each type.

   (2) An operator's licence shall not authorise the use of any vehicle unless the place which is for the time being its operating centre—

   (a) is in the area of the licensing authority by whom the licence was granted; or

   (b) is outside that area and has not been the operating centre of that vehicle for a period of more than three months.

For the purposes of paragraph (b) of this subsection, two or more successive periods which are not separated from each other by an interval of at least three months shall be treated as a single period having a duration equal to the total duration of those periods.

   (3) A motor vehicle which, after the grant of an operator's licence, is acquired by the holder of the licence, or comes into his possession under an agreement for hire-purchase, hire or loan, and thereupon becomes an authorised vehicle by virtue of subsection (1)(c) of this section, shall cease

to be an authorised vehicle on the expiration of one month from the date on which it was acquired by him or came into his possession unless before the expiration of that period he delivers to the licensing authority a notice in such form as the authority may require to the effect that the vehicle has been acquired by him, or has come into his possession, as the case may be.

(4) Where the licensing authority by whom a licence was granted receives a notice under subsection (3) of this section to the effect that the holder of the licence has acquired, or come into possession of, a vehicle as mentioned in that subsection, he shall, if the vehicle has become an authorised vehicle by virtue of subsection (1)(*c*) of this section, vary the licence by directing that the vehicle be specified therein.

(5) A motor vehicle specified in an operator's licence shall not, while it remains so specified, be capable of being effectively specified in any other operator's licence.

(6) Where it comes to the knowledge of the licensing authority by whom an operator's licence was granted that a vehicle specified therein—

> (*a*) has ceased to be used under the licence (otherwise than because of a fluctuation in business or because it is undergoing repair or maintenance); or
>
> (*b*) is specified in another operator's licence,

he may vary the licence by directing that the vehicle be removed therefrom.

62—(1) A person may apply for an operator's licence to the licensing authority for each area in which, if the licence is granted, the applicant will have an operating centre or operating centres; and a person may hold separate operators' licences in respect of different areas but shall not at any time hold more than one such licence in respect of the same area.

(2) A person applying for an operator's licence shall give to the licensing authority a statement giving such particulars as the authority may require of the motor vehicles proposed to be used under the licence which—

> (*a*) belong to the applicant, or
>
> (*b*) are in his possession under an agreement for hire-purchase, hire or loan, or
>
> (*c*) he intends, if the application is granted, to acquire, or to obtain possession of under such an agreement,

and also stating the number and type of any trailers proposed to be so used.

(3) A person applying for an operator's licence after the appointed day for the purposes of section 65 of this Act shall also give to the licensing authority a statement of the person or persons and of the other matters which he proposes should be specified in his licence for meeting the requirements of that section.

(4) A person applying for an operator's licence shall give to the licensing authority any further information which he may reasonably require for the discharge of his duties in relation to the application, and in particular shall, if he is required by the licensing authority so to do, give to him—

> (*a*) such particulars as he may require with respect to the purposes for which the vehicles referred to in the statement under subsection (2) of this section are proposed to be used;

(b) particulars of the arrangements for securing that Part VI of this Act (or, so long as those sections remain in force, sections 73 and 186 of the Act of 1960) will be complied with in the case of those vehicles, and for securing that those vehicles are not overloaded;

(c) particulars of the facilities and arrangements for securing that those vehicles will be maintained in a fit and serviceable condition;

(d) particulars of any activities carried on, at any time before the making of the application, by—

(i) the applicant,

(ii) any company of which the applicant is or has been a director;

(iii) where the applicant is a company, any person who is a director of the company;

(iv) where the applicant proposes to operate the said vehicles in partnership with other persons, any of those other persons;

(v) any company of which any such person as is mentioned in sub-paragraph (iii) or (iv) of this paragraph is or has been a director;

(vi) any company of which the applicant is a subsidiary,

being activities in carrying on any trade or business in the course of which vehicles of any description are operated, or as a person employed for the purposes of any such trade or business, or as a director of a company carrying on any such trade or business;

(e) particulars of any convictions during the five years preceding the making of the application—

(i) of the applicant; and

(ii) of any other person as to whose activities particulars may be required to be given under paragraph (d) of this subsection,

being convictions such as are mentioned in subsection (4) of section 69 of this Act (taking references in that subsection to the holder of the licence as references to the applicant or, as the case may be, to that other person);

(f) particulars of the financial resources which are or are likely to be available to the applicant;

(g) where the applicant is a company, the names of the directors and officers of the company, and of any company of which the first-mentioned company is a subsidiary, and where the authorised vehicles are proposed to be operated by the applicant in partnership with other persons, the names of those other persons.

(5) Any statement or information to be given to a licensing authority under this section shall be given in such form as the authority may require.

63—(1) Subject to subsection (2) of this section, the licensing authority shall publish in the prescribed manner notice of any application to the authority for an operator's licence.

(2) The licensing authority for any area shall not be obliged to publish

notice of any application made by a person who is the holder of an operator's licence granted by the licensing authority for any other area if satisfied that the grant of the application will not result in any increase in the number of authorised vehicles under operators' licences held by the applicant which is substantial having regard to the existing number of such vehicles.

(3) Any of the following persons, that is to say—

(a) a prescribed trade union or association, being a trade union or association whose members consist of or include—

(i) persons holding operator' licences or carriers' licences; or

(ii) employees of any such persons;

(b) a chief officer of police;

(c) a local authority,

may object to the grant of any application of which notice has been published under subsection (1) of this section on the ground that any of the requirements mentioned in section 64(2) of this Act are not satisfied in the case of the application.

(4) Any objection under this section shall be made within the prescribed time and in the prescribed manner (which shall be stated in the notice published under subsection (1) of this section) and shall contain particulars of the ground on which it is made.

(5) The onus of proof of the existence of the ground on which an objection is made shall lie on the objector.

(6) In this section—

"local authority" means—

(a) as respects England and Wales, the council of a county, county borough, county district or London borough, the Greater London Council and the Common Council of the City of London;

(b) as respects Scotland, a county council and a town council;

"trade union" has the same meaning as in the Trade Union Act 1913.

64—(1) On an application for an operator's licence, the licensing authority shall in every case consider whether the requirements mentioned in paragraphs (a) to (d) of subsection (2) of this section, and, if the licensing authority in any case thinks fit, paragraph (e) of that subsection, are satisfied, and in doing so shall have regard to any objection duly made under section 63 of this Act.

(2) The said requirements are as follows—

(a) that the applicant is a fit person to hold an operator's licence, having regard to the matters of which particulars may be required to be given under section 62(4)(d) and (e) of this Act;

(b) that the proposals in any statement furnished by the applicant under section 62(3) of this Act are satisfactory;

(c) that there will be satisfactory arrangements for securing that Part VI of this Act (or, so long as those sections remain in force, sections 73 and 186 of the Act of 1960) will be complied with in the case of the authorised vehicles, and for securing that those vehicles are not overloaded;

(*d*) that there will be satisfactory facilities and arrangements for maintaining the authorised vehicles in a fit and serviceable condition;

(*e*) that the provision of such facilities and arrangements as are mentioned in paragraph (*d*) of this subsection will not be prejudiced by reason of the applicant's having insufficient financial resources for that purpose.

(3) If the licensing authority determines that any requirement which he has taken into consideration in accordance with subsection (1) of this section is not satisfied, he shall refuse the application but, in any other case, he shall, subject to subsection (4) of this section, grant the application.

(4) In any case in which the licensing authority grants an application for an operator's licence, the licensing authority may issue that licence in the terms applied for or, if the authority thinks fit, subject to either or both of the following modifications or limitations, that is to say—

(*a*) so that the licence is in respect of motor vehicles other than those of which particulars were contained in the application, or in respect of motor vehicles or trailers greater or less in number than, or differing in type from, those for the use of which authorisation was applied for;

(*b*) so that the licence does not permit the addition of authorised vehicles under section 61(1)(*c*) of this Act.

(5) In exercising his functions under this section in relation to the requirement mentioned in subsection (2)(*e*) thereof, a licensing authority may be assisted by an assessor drawn from a panel of persons appointed by the Minister for that purpose; and there shall be paid by the licensing authority to any such assessor in respect of his services remuneration on a scale prescribed by the Minister with the approval of the Treasury.

65—(1) In every operator's licence granted by a licensing authority on an application made after the appointed day for the purposes of this section there shall be specified, in relation to each place in the area of the authority which, when the licence is granted, will be an operating centre of the holder of the licence, a person (being the holder of the licence, if an individual, or a person employed by him) who is to be responsible for the operation and maintenance of the authorised vehicles normally used from that centre, and it shall be a condition of the licence—

(*a*) that the person so specified shall be the holder of a transport manager's licence of the prescribed class; and

(*b*) if the person so specified is an employee of the holder of the operator's licence, that that person is employed by him in a position of responsibility specified in the licence.

(2) Where, at any time after an operators' licence has been granted as mentioned in subsection (1) of this section by the licensing authority for any area, a place in that area becomes an operating centre of the holder of the licence, that subsection shall, at the expiration of the period of three months beginning at that time, apply to the new operating centre as it applies to any operating centre which the holder of the licence has when the licence is granted.

161

(3) Unless in any case the licensing authority in his discretion otherwise determines, the person specified in any licence for the purposes of subsection (1) of this section in relation to any operating centre of any person shall not be the same as the person specified for those purposes in relation to any other operating centre of that person, whether in that licence or in any other operator's licence which is then held by him.

(4) The licensing authority may, if he thinks fit, permit the responsibility for the operation and maintenance of the authorised vehicles normally used from any particular operating centre to be shared between two or more persons; and, in any such case, subsection (1) of this section shall have effect—

> (a) as if it required both or all of those persons to be specified in the licence, together with the manner in which the responsibility is to be shared between them; and
>
> (b) as if references in paragraphs (a) and (b) to the person specified in the licence were references to each of the persons so specified by virtue of this subsection.

(5) In specifying for the purposes of subsection (1) of this section a position of responsibility to be held by any person, the licensing authority shall secure that that person thereby carries direct responsibility for the operation and maintenance of the authorised vehicles normally used from the operating centre in question or such share of that responsibility as may have been allocated to him under the last foregoing subsection.

(6) For the purposes of subsection (1) of this section a director of a company shall be deemed to be employed by it; and where the authorised vehicles are to be operated by the holder of an operator's licence in partnership with other persons, any of those other persons may be specified in the licence for the purposes of that subsection, but, if any of them is so specified, it shall be an additional condition of the licence that the authorised vehicles are operated by the holder of the licence in partnership with the person so specified.

(7) Where at any time a person specified in an operator's licence for the purposes of any condition imposed by or under this section dies, or ceases to be employed by the holder of the licence in a position of responsibility specified therein, or ceases to hold a transport manager's licence of the prescribed class, or any other event occurs whereby such a condition is contravened, that condition shall nevertheless be deemed not to have been contravened—

> (a) during the period of three months beginning at that time or such longer period as the licensing authority who issued the operator's licence may in any particular case allow; and
>
> (b) if before the expiration of that period the holder of the operator's licence duly applies for the licence to be varied for the purpose of bringing the contravention to an end, during the period until the application, and any appeal arising out of it, have been disposed of.

(8) The Minister may by regulations—

> (a) modify the requirements of subsections (1) to (6) of this section in any respect, or substitute for any of them such other require-

ments relating to transport managers' licences as may be specified in the regulations;

(*b*) substitute for the period of three months mentioned in subsection (7)(*a*) of this section such longer period as may be specified in the regulations;

and such regulations may make different provision for different cases and may contain such transitional and supplementary provisions as the Minister thinks necessary or expedient.

(9) Subject to subsection (7) of this section, any person who uses an authorised vehicle from an operating centre of his for a purpose for which it cannot lawfully be used without the authority of an operator's licence—

(*a*) at a time when a condition under this section of an operator's licence held by him is contravened in relation to that operating centre; or

(*b*) at a time when the matters required by virtue of subsection (1) or (2) of this section to be specified in relation to that operating centre in an operator's licence held by him are not so specified,

shall be liable on summary conviction to a fine not exceeding £200.

(10) Schedule 9 to this Act shall have effect in relation to transport managers' licences.

(11) In this section references to responsibility for the operation of any vehicles include (without prejudice to the generality of that expression) references to responsibility for securing that the drivers of the vehicles are properly licensed and comply with Part VI of this Act or, so long as those sections remain in force, sections 73 and 186 of the Act of 1960.

66—(1) A licensing authority, in granting an operator's licence, may attach thereto such conditions as he thinks fit for requiring the holder to inform him—

(*a*) of any change, of a kind specified in the conditions, in the organisation, management or ownership of the trade or business in the course of which the authorised vehicles are used;

(*b*) where the holder of the licence is a company, of any change, or of any change of a kind so specified, in the persons holding shares in the company;

(*c*) of any other event of a kind so specified affecting the holder of the licence which is relevant to the exercise of any powers of the authority in relation to the licence.

(2) Any person who contravenes any condition attached under this section to a licence of which he is the holder shall be liable on summary conviction to a fine not exceeding £200.

67—(1) There shall be specified in every operator's licence the date on which the licence is to come into force.

(2) Regulations may specify the dates in the year on which operators' licences shall expire, and, subject to subsections (4) and (5) of this section, an operator's licence shall, unless previously revoked, continue in force up till and including that one of the specified dates which occurs next before the expiration of the period of five years beginning with the date on which the licence came into force, or of such other period beginning with that

date as the licensing authority may in accordance with the next following subsection direct.

(3) The licensing authority may, on granting an operator's licence, direct that in the case of that licence the period relevant for the purposes of subsection (2) of this section—

(a) shall be a period shorter than five years—
  (i) if the applicant for the licence so requests; or
  (ii) if the application is made by a person who does not hold an operator's licence when the application is made;

(b) shall be a period longer or shorter than five years if the licensing authority is of opinion that it is desirable so to direct in order to arrange a suitable and convenient programme of work for the licensing authority.

(4) If, at the date on which an operator's licence is due to expire, proceedings are pending before the licensing authority on an application by the holder of that licence for the grant to him of a new licence in substitution therefor, the existing licence shall continue in force until—

(a) the application; and

(b) any appeal under section 70 of this Act arising out of the application,

are disposed of, without prejudice, however, to the exercise in the meantime of the powers conferred by section 69 of this Act.

(5) If an applicant for an operator's licence so requests, a licensing authority may, if the applicant does not hold an operator's licence granted by that authority, grant to him, pending the determination of the application, an operator's licence expressed to continue in force until the date on which any licence granted on the application or on an appeal arising out of it is expressed to come into force or, if no licence is granted as aforesaid, until the application is refused; and a request for the grant of a licence under this subsection shall not for the purposes of section 63 or 64 of this Act be treated as an application for an operator's licence, and a licence granted under this subsection shall not for the purposes of section 65 of this Act be treated as an operator's licence.

68—(1) On the application of the holder of an operator's licence, the licensing authority by whom the licence was granted may at any time while it is in force vary the licence by directing—

(a) that additional vehicles be specified therein, that the maximum number of trailers or of motor vehicles specified therein under paragraph (b) or (c) of section 61(1) of this Act be increased, or, if the licence does not permit the addition of authorised vehicles under the said paragraph (c), that it shall so permit and that a maximum be specified under that paragraph accordingly; or

(b) that vehicles specified therein be removed therefrom or that any such maximum as is mentioned in paragraph (a) of this subsection be reduced; or

(c) that an alteration or addition be made in or to any of the matters specified in the licence for the purposes of section 65 of this Act; or

164

(*d*) that an alteration be made in any condition attached to the licence under section 66 of this Act or that any such condition be removed.

(2) A person applying for a direction under this section shall give to the licensing authority such information as he may reasonably require for the discharge of his duties in relation to the application.

(3) Any information or particulars to be given to a licensing authority under subsection (2) of this section shall be given in such form as the authority may require.

(4) Except in the following cases, that is to say—

    (*a*) where the application is for a direction under subsection (1)(*a*) of this section and the licensing authority is satisfied that, if the application were an application under section 63 of this Act, no notice of it would be required to be published by virtue of subsection (2) of that section; or

    (*b*) where the application is for a direction under subsection (1)(*b*) of this section; or

    (*c*) where the licensing authority is satisfied that the application is of so trivial a nature that it is not necessary that an opportunity should be given for objecting to it,

the licensing authority shall publish notice of any application under this section in the manner provided for the publication of notices under subsection (1) of the said section 63; and where notice of the application is published in pursuance of this subsection the other provisions of the said section 63 and the provisions of section 64 of this Act shall, so far as applicable and subject to any necessary modifications, apply to that application as they apply to an application for the grant of an operator's licence of which notice is published under subsection (1) of the said section 63.

(5) If an applicant under this section so requests, the licensing authority may, pending the determination of the application, give an interim direction under this section, that is to say, a direction expressed to continue in force only until the application, and any appeal arising out of it, have been disposed of; and a request for such a direction shall not for the purposes of subsection (4) of this section be treated as an application under this section.

69—(1) Subject to the provisions of this section, the licensing authority by whom an operator's licence was granted may direct that it be revoked, suspended or curtailed on any of the following grounds—

    (*a*) that the holder of the licence has contravened section 65 of this Act or any condition attached to his licence under section 66 of this Act;

    (*b*) that during the five years ending with the date on which the direction is given there has been (whether before or after the day on which this section comes into force)—

        (i) any such conviction as is mentioned in paragraphs (*a*) to (*f*) of subsection (4) of this section or any such prohibition as is mentioned in paragraph (*h*) of that subsection; or

        (ii) any such conviction as is mentioned in paragraph (*g*) of that subsection on occasions appearing to the licensing authority to be sufficiently numerous to justify the giving of a direction under this subsection;

(c) that the holder of the licence made or procured to be made for the purposes of his application for the licence, or for the purposes of an application for the variation of the licence, a statement of fact which (whether to his knowledge or not) was false, or a statement of intention or expectation which has not been fulfilled;

(d) that the holder of the licence has been adjudicated bankrupt or, where the holder is a company, has gone into liquidation (not being a voluntary liquidation for the purpose of reconstruction);

(e) that there has been since the licence was granted or varied a material change in any of the circumstances of the holder of the licence which were relevant to the grant or variation of his licence;

(f) that the licence is liable to revocation, suspension or curtailment by virtue of a direction under subsection (6) of this section;

and during any time of suspension the licence shall be of no effect.

(2) In any case in which a licensing authority has power to give a direction under the foregoing subsection in respect of any licence, the authority shall also have power to direct that there be attached to the licence any, or any additional, condition such as is mentioned in section 66 of this Act.

(3) Where the existence of any of the grounds mentioned in subsection (1) of this section is brought to the notice of the licensing authority in the case of the holder of any licence granted by him, the authority shall consider whether or not to give a direction under this section in respect of that licence.

(4) The convictions and prohibitions mentioned in subsection (1)(b) of this section are as follows—

(a) a conviction, in relation to a goods vehicle, of the holder of the licence, or a servant or agent of his, of contravening any provision (however expressed) contained in or having effect under any enactment (including any enactment passed after this Act) relating to—

(i) the maintenance of vehicles in a fit and serviceable condition;

(ii) limits of speed and weight laden and unladen, and the loading of good vehicles;

(iii) the licensing of drivers:

(b) a conviction of the holder of the licence under—

(i) this Part of this Act or Schedule 9 thereto;

(ii) section 233 or 235 of the Act of 1960 so far as applicable (by virtue of Schedule 10 to this Act) to licences, authorisations or means of identification under this Part of this Act or Schedule 9 thereto;

(iii) any regulation made under this Act which is prescribed for the purposes of this subsection;

166

(c) a conviction, in relation to a goods vehicle, of the holder of the licence or a servant or agent of his under, or of conspiracy to contravene, Part VI of this Act or section 73 or 186 of the Act of 1960;

(d) a conviction of the holder of the licence under section 7 of the Road Haulage Wages Act 1938 (which makes failure to pay the statutory remuneration under that Act an offence);

(e) a conviction, in relation to a goods vehicle, of the holder of the licence under, or of conspiracy to contravene, section 200 of the Customs and Excise Act 1952 (unlawful use of rebated fuel oil);

(f) a conviction of the holder of the licence under section 18 of the Road Safety Act 1967 (operator's duty to inspect, and keep records of inspection of, goods vehicles);

(g) a conviction, in relation to a goods vehicle, of the holder of the licence, or a servant or agent of his, of contravening any provision (however expressed) which prohibits or restricts the waiting of vehicles, being a provision contained in an order made under section 1, 6, 9 or 11 of the Road Traffic Regulation Act 1967 (including any such order made by virtue of section 84A(2) of that Act) or under any enactment repealed by that Act and re-enacted by any of those sections;

(h) a prohibition of the use of a vehicle under section 184 of the Act of 1960 or of the driving of a vehicle under section 16 of the Road Safety Act 1967, being a vehicle of which the holder of the licence was the owner when the prohibition was imposed.

(5) Where the licensing authority directs that an operator's licence be revoked, the authority may order the person who was the holder thereof to be disqualified, indefinitely or for such period as the authority thinks fit, from holding or obtaining an operator's licence, and so long as the disqualification is in force—

(a) notwithstanding anything in section 64 of this Act, no operator's licence shall be granted to him and any operator's licence obtained by him shall be of no effect; and

(b) if he applies for or obtains an operator's licence he shall be liable on summary conviction to a fine not exceeding £200.

An order under this subsection may be limited so as to apply only to the holding or obtaining of an operator's licence in respect of the area of one or more specified licensing authorities and, if the order is so limited, paragraphs (a) and (b) of this subsection shall apply only to any operator's licence to which the order applies; but, notwithstanding section 61(2)(b) of this Act, no other operator's licence held by the person in question shall authorise the use by him of any vehicle at a time when its operating centre is in an area in respect of which he is disqualified by virtue of the order.

(6) Where the licensing authority makes an order under subsection (5) of this section in respect of any person, the authority may direct that if that person, at any time or during such period as the authority may specify—

(a) is a director of, or holds a controlling interest in—

(i) a company which holds a licence of the kind to which the order in question applies; or

(ii) a company of which such a company as aforesaid is a subsidiary; or

(b) operates any goods vehicles in partnership with a person who holds such a licence,

that licence of that company, or, as the case may be, of that person, shall be liable to revocation, suspension or curtailment under this section.

(7) The powers conferred by subsections (5) and (6) of this section in relation to the person who was the holder of a licence shall be exercisable also, where that person was a company, in relation to any director of that company, and, where that person operated the authorised vehicles in partnership with other persons, in relation to any of those other persons.

(8) A licensing authority who has made an order or given a direction under subsection (5), (6) or (7) of this section may, in such circumstances as may be prescribed, cancel that order or direction.

(9) A licensing authority shall not—

(a) give a direction under subsection (1) or (2) of this section in respect of any licence; or

(b) make an order or give a direction under subsection (5), (6) or (7) of this section in respect of any person,

without first holding an inquiry if the holder of the licence or that person, as the case may be, requests him to do so.

(10) The licensing authority may direct that any direction or order given or made by him under subsection (1), (2), (5), (6) or (7) of this section shall not take effect until the expiration of the time within which an appeal may be made to the Transport Tribunal against the direction or order and, if such an appeal is made, until the appeal has been disposed of; and if the licensing authority refuses to give a direction under this subsection the holder of the licence, or, as the case may be, the person in respect of whom the direction or order was given or made under any of those subsections, may apply to the tribunal for such a direction, and the tribunal shall give its decision on the application within fourteen days.

(11) For the purposes of this section a person holds a controlling interest in a company if he is the beneficial owner of more than half its equity share capital as defined in section 154(5) of the Companies Act 1948.

70—(1) Subject to subsection (2) of this section, a person who—

(a) being an applicant for, or for the variation of, an operator's licence, is aggrieved by the refusal of the application or, as the case may be, by the terms or conditions of the licence or of the variation; or

(b) being the holder of an operator's licence in respect of which, or a person in respect of whom, a direction or order has been given or made under section 61(6) or 69(1) to (7) of this Act, is aggrieved by that direction or order; or

(c) having duly made an objection to an application for, or for the

168

variation of, an operator's licence, is aggrieved by the grant of the application,
may appeal to the Transport Tribunal.

(2) No appeal shall lie under the foregoing subsection on the ground that a direction has been given under subsection (3) of section 67 of this Act if it has been given by virtue of paragraph (*b*) of the said subsection (3).

Special authorisations for use of large goods vehicles

71—(1) Subject to the provisions of this section and to the other provisions of this Part of this Act, no person shall, after the appointed day for the purposes of this section, use a large goods vehicle on a road—

(*a*) to carry any goods on, or on any part of, a controlled journey; or

(*b*) to carry an amount exceeding eleven tons in weight of any prescribed goods otherwise than on a controlled journey,

except under a special authorisation granted under this Part of this Act.

(2) For the purposes of the foregoing subsection, a controlled journey is a journey between places in Great Britain separated by a distance exceeding one hundred miles, being—

(*a*) in relation to goods to which paragraph (*b*) of this subsection does not apply, a journey for the whole of which the goods are carried on the same large goods vehicle without being taken off it;

(*b*) in relation to goods in a container having a volume (ascertained by external measurement) of not less than six hundred cubic feet or on a pallet having a surface area of not less than fifty square feet, a journey for every part of which they are carried by a large goods vehicle (whether the same vehicle or successive vehicles) without being taken out of the container or off the pallet;

and, where the vehicle on which the goods are carried is a trailer, it is immaterial whether it is drawn on the journey by the same vehicle or different vehicles.

(3) For the purposes of this section goods shall be treated as carried on a vehicle notwithstanding the fact that the vehicle is itself being carried on a vessel, aircraft or other means of transport, but, in relation to a journey in the course of which a vehicle is so carried, the distance to be taken into account for the purposes of subsection (2) of this section shall be the aggregate of the distances separating the points between which the vehicle is not so carried on the journey.

(4) Where in the case of any controlled journey—

(*a*) no one person uses a vehicle or vehicles to carry the goods in question between places separated by a distance exceeding one hundred miles; and

(*b*) a special authorisation applicable to that journey is held by any one of the persons who use a vehicle or vehicles to carry those goods in the course of that journey,

then, if under that authorisation the journey is one which may be undertaken in part by persons other than the holder of the licence, it shall not be necessary for the purposes of subsection (1)(*a*) of this section for any of those other persons to hold a special authorisation.

(5) The Minister may by regulations direct—
  (a) that subsection (1) of this section shall not apply—
    (i) to carriage on journeys in the case of which the distances specified in the regulations are not exceeded;
    (ii) to carriage by vehicles of any class specified in the regulations;
  (b) that paragraph (a) of that subsection shall not apply to the carriage of any prescribed goods;
and regulations under paragraph (b) of this subsection or prescribing goods for the purposes of subsection (1)(b) of this section may describe the goods in question by reference to their nature, to the amount in which, or the places between which, they are carried, or by reference to any other circumstances.

(6) For the purposes of this section and the subsequent provisions of this Part of this Act, a large goods vehicle is a goods vehicle (other than a hauling vehicle) which—
  (a) has a relevant plated weight exceeding sixteen tons or (not having a relevant plated weight) has an unladen weight exceeding five tons; or
  (b) forms part of a vehicle combination (not being an articulated combination) which is such that—
    (i) if all the vehicles comprised in the combination (or all of them except any small trailer) have relevant plated weights, the aggregate of the relevant plated weights of the vehicles comprised in the combination (exclusive of any such trailer) exceeds sixteen tons;
    (ii) in any other case, the aggregate of the unladen weights of those vehicles (exclusive of any such trailer) exceeds five tons; or
  (c) forms part of an articulated combination which is such that—
    (i) if the trailer comprised in the combination has a relevant plated weight, the aggregate of the unladen weight of the motor vehicle comprised in the combination and the relevant plated weight of that trailer exceeds sixteen tons;
    (ii) in any other case, the aggregate of the unladen weights of the motor vehicle and the trailer comprised in the combination exceeds five tons.

In any provision of this subsection "relevant plated weight" means a plated weight of the description specified in relation to that provision by regulations; and in paragraph (b) of this subsection "small trailer" means a trailer having an unladen weight not exceeding one ton.

(7) Subsection (1)(b) of this section shall apply to the carriage of an amount exceeding eleven tons in weight of any prescribed goods in two or more vehicles forming part of a vehicle combination such as is mentioned in subsection (6)(b) or (c) of this section as it applies to the carriage of such an amount in a single vehicle, whether forming part of such a combination or not.

(8) In this section—

"hauling vehicle" means a motor tractor, a light locomotive, a heavy locomotive or the motor vehicle comprised in an articulated combination;

"pallet" means a moveable deck on which a quantity of goods can be assembled for the purpose of being handled, loaded or transported as a single unit, and "surface area" in relation to a pallet means the area on which the goods can be assembled as aforesaid.

(9) Nothing in this section shall apply to the use of a vehicle by any person for the carriage of goods otherwise than for hire or reward or for or in connection with any trade or business carried on by him.

(10) Any person who uses a vehicle in contravention of this section shall be liable on summary conviction to a fine not exceeding £200.

72—(1) An application for a special authorisation shall be made to the licensing authority for the area containing the operating centre or operating centres of the vehicles proposed to be used under the authorisation.

(2) An application for a special authorisation shall be made in such form as the licensing authority may require, and shall contain a statement giving such particulars as the licensing authority may require—

(a) of the vehicles proposed to be used under the authorisation; and

(b) of the transport service proposed to be provided under the authorisation, that is to say—

(i) the goods proposed to be carried;

(ii) the places between which they are to be carried;

(iii) the person or persons (so far as known) for whom they are to be carried; and

(iv) where applicable, the occasions on which or the circumstances in which they are to be carried.

(3) In subsection (2)(b)(iii) of this section references to the person or persons for whom any goods are to be carried are references, if the goods are to be carried for hire or reward, to the person or persons for whom they are to be so carried, and, if the goods are to be carried by any person for or in connection with any trade or business carried on by him, to that person.

73—(1) Where a licensing authority receives an application for a special authorisation, the authority shall, subject to subsection (2) of this section and to section 75 of this Act, send a copy of the application to the Railways Board and, unless the application is made by the Freight Corporation, to that Corporation.

(2) Where an application for a special authorisation is accompanied by a statement signed by a person on behalf of the Railways Board or the Freight Corporation to the effect that the body in question has no objection to the application, no copy of the application shall be sent to that body under subsection (1) of this section; and where an application for a special authorisation is made solely for the purpose of section 71(1)(b) of this Act, no copy of the application shall be sent to the Freight Corporation.

(3) Within fourteen days of the date on which a copy of an application for a special authorisation is sent to either of the said bodies under subsection (1) of this section that body may, by a notice sent to the

171

licensing authority and the applicant, object to the grant of the application—

    (*a*) in respect of the whole of the transport service proposed to be provided in pursuance of the special authorisation; or

    (*b*) in respect of any part of that service,

on the ground that the service or part can be provided by that body, or by a subsidiary of that body, wholly or partly by rail.

(4) A service or part of a service to which an objection under this section relates is hereafter in this Part of this Act referred to as "the disputed service."

(5) If an objection is duly made under this section—

    (*a*) the body making the objection shall submit to the licensing authority a statement containing particulars of the manner in which, and the charges at which, the disputed service can be provided by that body, or by a subsidiary of that body, wholly or partly by rail, and of any other matters on which that body relies for the purposes of the objection;

    (*b*) the applicant shall submit to the licensing authority a statement containing particulars of the grounds on which he relies in support of his application;

and, unless on a consideration of those statements it appears to the licensing authority that the application can, without further investigation, be granted in accordance with section 74 of this Act in respect of the whole of the disputed service, the licensing authority shall, before coming to a decision on the application, send to the applicant and the objector a copy of the statement submitted by the other party and hold an inquiry.

(6) Any statement to be submitted to a licensing authority under this section shall be submitted within such time and shall be in such form as the licensing authority may require.

    74—(1) If no objection to an application is duly made under section 73 of this Act, or if such an objection is duly made under subsection (3)(*b*) of that section, the licensing authority shall, subject to subsection (7) of this section, grant the application or, as the case may be, grant it in respect of the part of the transport service to which the objection does not relate.

(2) If an objection to an application is duly made under the said section 73, the licensing authority—

    (*a*) shall grant the application in respect of the whole of the disputed service if satisfied that the condition mentioned in subsection (3) of this section is fulfilled in the case of the whole of the disputed service;

    (*b*) shall grant the application in respect of any part of the disputed service if satisfied that the said condition is fulfilled in the case of that part;

but, save as aforesaid and subject to subsection (4) of this section, the licensing authority shall refuse the application.

(3) The condition referred to in subsection (2) of this section is that the provision of the disputed service, or of the part of that service in question,

172

by the objector, or a subsidiary of the objector, wholly or partly by rail, as compared with its provision in pursuance of the special authorisation, will be less advantageous for the person for whom the goods in question are to be carried.

(4) If in the case of the whole or any part of the disputed service the licensing authority is not satisfied as mentioned in subsection (2) of this section, the authority shall nevertheless grant the application in respect of the disputed service or of any part of it if satisfied—

    (*a*) that the provision of the service, or of that part of it, by the objector, or a subsidiary of the objector, wholly or partly by rail, as compared with its provision in pursuance of the special authorisation, will be equally advantageous for the person for whom the goods in question are to be carried; and

    (*b*) that, if a special authorisation is not granted for the provision of the service or the part of it in question, serious detriment will result to a person (whether the applicant himself or some other person) for whom the applicant provides or proposes to provide a transport service other than the disputed service or other than the part of it in question.

(5) The factors relevant for making the comparison mentioned in subsections (3) and (4)(*a*) of this section shall be speed, reliability, cost, and such other matters relevant to the needs of the person for whom the goods in question are to be carried as may be prescribed; and the licensing authority shall assess the relative importance of those factors by reference to the needs of the person for whom the goods in question are to be carried and to the nature of those goods.

(6) In assessing the factors mentioned in subsection (5) of this section and the detriment mentioned in subsection (4)(*b*) of this section the licensing authority shall act in accordance with any directions contained in regulations made by the Minister.

(7) Where an application for a special authorisation is made by the Freight Corporation and no objection to it is made by the Railways Board, or where such an application is made by a subsidiary of that Corporation and no objection to it is made by that Board or by the Corporation, the licensing authority to whom the application is made shall grant the application only if and so far as he considers that it would have been granted if any objection reasonably open to the Board or, as the case may be, to the Board or the Corporation, had been made by them; and the licensing authority may for that purpose require the Board and the Corporation to give him such information and explanations as he may reasonably require.

(8) In exercising his functions under this section, a licensing authority may be assisted by an assessor drawn from a panel of persons appointed by the Minister for that purpose; and there shall be paid by the licensing authority to any such assessor in respect of his services remuneration on a scale prescribed by the Minister with the approval of the Treasury.

(9) In this section references to the person for whom any goods are to be carried are references, if the goods are to be carried for hire or reward,

to the person for whom they are to be so carried, and, if the goods are to be carried by any person for or in connection with any trade or business carried on by him, to that person; and, subject to regulations under subsection (6) of this section, references to the cost of carrying any goods are references, where they are carried for hire or reward, to the charges made for their carriage and, where they are not so carried, to the cost of carrying them.

75—(1) If, on an application to a licensing authority for a special authorisation, it appears to the authority—

(a) that the application is made solely for the purpose of enabling the applicant to provide a transport service in circumstances which he could not reasonably have foreseen; and

(b) that by reason of the urgency of the case the purposes of the application would be defeated if it were dealt with in accordance with section 73 of this Act,

the licensing authority may grant that application without reference to that section if and so far as he considers that no objection to the application could reasonably have been made under that section or that any such objection could not reasonably have succeeded.

(2) Any special authorisation granted by virtue of this section shall expire at the end of the period of three months beginning with the date on which it comes into force or of such shorter period beginning with that date as the licensing authority may direct.

76—(1) In granting a special authorisation the licensing authority shall attach thereto such conditions as he thinks requisite for defining the transport service which is authorised by the special authorisation, and may attach thereto such other conditions as he thinks fit, including in particular conditions—

(a) as to the vehicles which may be used under the special authorisation;

(b) requiring the holder of the authorisation to make and preserve records as to his operations in pursuance of the authorisation;

(c) requiring the holder of the authorisation to secure that a copy of the conditions defining the transport service authorised by the authorisation is carried by the driver of any vehicle used by him for a purpose for which such an authorisation is required.

(2) In granting a special authorisation for the purposes of section 71(1)(a) of this Act the licensing authority shall include in the authorisation a statement as to whether any controlled journeys authorised by the authorisation may be undertaken in part by persons other than the holder of the authorisation; and, if the statement permits such journeys to be undertaken as aforesaid, the licensing authority may specify conditions to be observed by persons other than the holder of the licence who undertake such journeys.

(3) Any person who contravenes any condition attached under this section to a special authorisation of which he is the holder, or, being a person who undertakes part of a controlled journey by virtue of a statement included in a special authorisation under subsection (2) of this section,

contravenes any condition specified under that subsection, shall be liable on summary conviction to a fine not exceeding £200.

77—(1) There shall be specified in every special authorisation the date on which the authorisation is to come into force.

(2) Regulations may specify the dates in the year on which special authorisations shall expire, and, subject to subsections (3) and (4) of this section, a special authorisation shall, unless previously revoked, continue in force up till and including that one of the specified dates which occurs next before the expiration of the period of five years beginning with the date on which the authorisation came into force or of such shorter period beginning with that date as the licensing authority may direct.

(3) If at the date on which a special authorisation is due to expire, proceedings are pending before the licensing authority on an application by the holder of that authorisation for the grant to him of a new authorisation in substitution therefore, the existing authorisation shall continue in force until—

(a) that application; and
(b) any appeal under section 80 of this Act arising out of the application,

are disposed of, without prejudice however to the exercise in the meantime of the powers conferred by section 79 of this Act.

(4) Nothing in this section shall preclude the grant of a special authorisation authorising the carriage of goods only on occasions or in circumstances specified in the authorisation: and subsection (2) of this section shall not apply to any special authorisation granted by virtue of section 75 of this Act.

78—(1) The holder of a special authorisation may at any time while it is in force apply to the licensing authority by whom it was granted for a variation thereof so as to permit him to provide under it a transport service differing in any respect from that already authorised thereby or for a variation of any condition attached to the licence under subsection (1) of section 76 of this Act or of any statement included in it under, or of any condition specified by virtue of, subsection (2) of that section.

(2) Subsections (2) and (3) of section 72 of this Act shall, so far as applicable and subject to any necessary modifications, apply to any application under this section as they apply to an application for a special authorisation.

(3) Where a licensing authority receives an application under this section, the authority (unless satisfied that the grant of the application would not result in any material change in the transport service already authorised by the special authorisation) shall send copies of the application to any body to which they would be required to be sent under subsection (1) of section 73 of this Act if the application were an application under that section; and where copies of the application are so sent in pursuance of this subsection, the other provisions of that section and the provisions of section 74 of this Act shall, so far as applicable and subject to any necessary modifications, apply to that application as they apply to an application for a special authorisation.

79—(1) Subject to the provisions of this section, the licensing authority by whom a special authorisation was granted may direct that it be revoked or suspended on the ground—

(a) that the holder has contravened section 71 of this Act by using a large goods vehicle otherwise than as permitted by the authorisation or has contravened any condition attached to the authorisation under section 76 of this Act;

(b) that since the authorisation was granted the holder has been convicted under section 81(4) of this Act;

(c) that the holder of the authorisation made or procured to be made for the purposes of his application for the authorisation, or for the purposes of an application for the variation of the authorisation, a statement of fact which (whether to his knowledge or not) was false, or a statement of intention or expectation which has not been fulfilled; or

(d) that there has been since the authorisation was granted or varied a material change in any of the circumstances of the holder of the authorisation which were relevant to the grant or variation of the authorisation;

and during any time of suspension the authorisation shall be of no effect.

(2) In any case in which a licensing authority has power to give a direction under subsection (1) of this section in respect of any authorisation, the authority shall also have power to direct that any alteration be made in its terms so as to restrict in any respect the transport service which it authorises, or that there be attached to the authorisation any, or any additional, condition such as is mentioned in section 76 of this Act, or that any such condition be altered.

(3) Where the licensing authority directs that a special authorisation be revoked, the authority may order the person who was the holder thereof to be disqualified, indefinitely or for such period as the authority thinks fit, from holding or obtaining a special authorisation, and so long as the disqualification is in force—

(a) notwithstanding anything in section 74 or 75 of this Act, no special authorisation shall be granted to him and any special authorisation obtained by him shall be of no effect; and

(b) if he applies for or obtains a special authorisation he shall be liable on summary conviction to a fine not exceeding £200.

An order under this subsection may be limited so as to apply only to the holding or obtaining of a special authorisation in respect of the area of one or more specified licensing authorities and, if the order is so limited, paragraphs (a) and (b) of this subsection shall apply only to any special authorisation to which the order applies.

(4) A licensing authority who has made an order under subsection (3) of this section may, in such circumstances as may be prescribed, cancel that order.

(5) Where the licensing authority gives a direction under this section in respect of a special authorisation held by any person, the authority may also direct that any operator's licence held by that person be revoked,

176

suspended or curtailed and, if he directs that it be revoked, may exercise the powers conferred by section 69(5) to (7) of this Act; and the provisions of section 69(8), (9) and (10) and of section 70(1)(*b*) of this Act shall apply to any direction or order given or made under or by virtue of this subsection as they apply to any direction or order given or made under any provision of section 69 of this Act.

(6) The licensing authority shall not exercise any of his powers under subsection (1), (2) or (3) of this section in respect of any authorisation or the holder of any authorisation without first holding an inquiry, if the holder of the authorisation requests him to do so.

(7) The licensing authority may direct that any direction or order given or made by him under subsection (1), (2) or (3) of this section shall not take effect until the expiration of the time within which an appeal may be made to the Transport Tribunal against the direction or order and, if such an appeal is made, until the appeal has been disposed of; and if the licensing authority refuses to give a direction under this subsection the holder of the authorisation may apply to the tribunal for such a direction, and the tribunal shall give its decision on the application within fourteen days.

80—(1) Subject to subsection (2) of this section, a person who—

(*a*) being an applicant for, or for the variation of, a special authorisation, is aggrieved by the refusal of the application or, as the case may be, by the terms or conditions of the authorisation or of the variation; or

(*b*) being the holder of a special authorisation in respect of which, or a person in respect of whom, a direction or order has been given or made under section 79(1), (2) or (3) of this Act, is aggrieved by that direction or order; or

(*c*) having duly made an objection to an application for, or for the variation of, a special authorisation, is aggrieved by the grant of the application,

may appeal to the Transport Tribunal.

(2) No appeal shall lie under subsection (1) of this section on the ground that a direction has been given under section 77(2) of this Act in the case of a special authorisation granted to any person if the effect of the direction is that the authorisation will expire on the same day as an operator's licence held by that person.

Enforcement

81—(1) Subject to subsection (2) of this section, no goods shall be carried on a large goods vehicle unless a document (in this section referred to as a "consignment note") in the prescribed form and containing the prescribed particulars has been completed and signed in the prescribed manner and is carried by the driver of the vehicle.

(2) Subsection (1) of this section shall not apply—

(*a*) to the carriage of goods on any journey or in a vehicle of any class exempted from that subsection by regulations; or

(*b*) to any carriage of goods which is lawful without the authority of an operator's licence;

and, subject to the provisions of regulations, a licensing authority may dispense with the observance, as respects the carriage of goods under an operator's licence granted by him, of any requirement of that subsection, and may grant such a dispensation either generally, or as respects a particular vehicle, or as respects the use of vehicles for a particular purpose, but he shall not grant such a dispensation unless satisfied that it is not reasonably practicable for the requirement dispensed with to be observed.

(3) The consignment note relating to the goods carried by a vehicle on any journey shall, at the conclusion of that journey, be preserved for the prescribed period by the person who used the vehicle (or, if the journey was a controlled journey within the meaning of section 71 of this Act, the last vehicle) for carrying the goods on that journey.

(4) Any person who uses or drives a vehicle in contravention of subsection (1) of this section or who fails to comply with subsection (3) thereof shall be liable on summary conviction to a fine not exceeding £200.

82—(1) An officer may, on production if so required of his authority, require any person to produce and permit him to inspect and copy—

(a) any record or other document which is required by or under section 76 or 81 of this Act to be carried by that person as driver of a vehicle;

(b) any record or other document which that person is required by or under either of those sections to preserve;

and that record or document shall, if the officer so requires by notice in writing served on that person, be produced at the office of the licensing authority specified in the notice within such time (not being less than ten days) from the service of the notice as may be so specified.

(2) An officer may, on production if so required of his authority—

(a) at any time, enter any large goods vehicle and inspect that vehicle and any goods carried by it;

(b) at any time which is reasonable having regard to the circumstances of the case, enter any premises on which he has reason to believe that such a vehicle is kept or that any such records or documents as are mentioned in subsection (1) of this section are to be found, and inspect any such vehicle, and inspect and copy any such record or document, which he finds there.

(3) For the purpose of exercising his powers under subsection (1)(a) or (2)(a) of this section, an officer may detain the vehicle in question during such time as is required for the exercise of that power.

(4) An officer may, at any time which is reasonable having regard to the circumstances of the case, enter any premises of an applicant for an operator's licence or of the holder of such a licence and inspect any facilities on those premises for maintaining the authorised vehicles in a fit and serviceable condition.

(5) Any person who—

(a) fails to comply with any requirement under subsection (1) of this section; or

178

(b) obstructs an officer in the exercise of his powers under subsection (2), (3) or (4) of this section,

shall be liable on summary conviction to a fine not exceeding £100.

(6) If an officer has reason to believe that a document or article carried on or by the driver of a vehicle, or a document produced to him in pursuance of this Part of his Act or Schedule 9 thereto, is a document or article in relation to which an offence has been committed under—

(a) section 83 of this Act; or

(b) section 233 or 235 of the Act of 1960 as amended by Schedule 10 to this Act,

he may seize that document or article; and where a document or article is seized as aforesaid and within six months of the date on which it was seized no person has been charged since that date with an offence in relation to that document or article under any of those sections and that document or article is still detained, a magistrates' court shall, on an application made for the purpose by the driver or owner of the vehicle, by the person from whom the document was seized or by an officer, make such order respecting the disposal of the document or article and award such costs as the justice of the case may require.

(7) Any proceedings in Scotland under the last foregoing subsection shall be taken by way of summary application in the sheriff court; and in the application of that subsection to Scotland references to costs shall be construed as references to expenses.

(8) In this section "officer" means an examiner appointed under Part IV of the Act of 1960 and any person authorised for the purposes of this section by the licensing authority for any area.

(9) The powers conferred by this section on an officer as defined in subsection (8) of this section shall be exercisable also by a police constable who shall not, if wearing uniform, be required to produce any authority.

83 Any person who makes, or causes to be made, any record or other document required to be made under section 76 or 81 of this Act which he knows to be false or, with intent to deceive, alters or causes to be altered any such record or document shall be liable—

(a) on summary conviction, to a fine not exceeding £200;

(b) on conviction on indictment, to imprisonment for a term not exceeding two years.

84 In any proceedings for an offence under this Part of this Act or Schedule 9 thereto a certificate signed by or on behalf of a licensing authority and stating—

(a) that, on any date, a person was or was not the holder of an operator's licence, a special authorisation or a transport manager's licence granted by the authority;

(b) the dates of the coming into force and expiration of any such licence or authorisation granted by the authority;

(c) the terms and conditions of any operator's licence or special authorisation granted by the authority;

(d) that a person is by virtue of an order of the authority disqualified from holding or obtaining an operator's licence, a special authorisation of a transport manager's licence indefinitely or for a specified period;

(e) that a direction, having effect indefinitely or for a specified period, has been given by the licensing authority under section 69(6) of this Act in relation to any person;

(f) that, on any date or during any specified period, any such licence or authorisation granted by the authority was of no effect by reason of a direction that it be suspended,

shall be evidence, and in Scotland sufficient evidence, of the facts stated; and a certificate stating any of the matters aforesaid and purporting to be signed by or on behalf of a licensing authority shall be deemed to be so signed unless the contrary is proved.

Supplementary

85—(1) The Minister may by regulations make provision for the purpose of enabling any company, or other body corporate, which has one or more subsidiaries to hold—

(a) an operator's licence under which the authorised vehicles consist of or include vehicles belonging to or in the possession of any of its subsidiaries;

(b) a special authorisation under which the transport service to which it relates may be provided by any of its subsidiaries.

(2) Regulations under this section may modify or supplement any of the provisions of this Part of this Act or Schedules 9 and 10 thereto so far as appears to the Minister to be necessary or expedient for the purpose mentioned in subsection (1) of this section or in connection therewith, and may contain such other supplementary and incidental provisions as appear to the Minister to be requisite.

86 Subject to any provision made by regulations under section 85 of this Act, an operator's licence and a special authorisation shall not be capable of being transferred or assigned, but provision may be made by regulations for treating a person carrying on the trade or business of the holder of an operator's licence or special authorisation as if he were the holder thereof (for such purposes, for such period and to such extent as may be specified in the regulations), in the event of the death, incapacity, bankruptcy or liquidation of the holder, or of the appointment of a receiver or manager in relation to the trade or business.

(87, 88, 89, 90 Sections dealing with the procedures for inquiries held by a licensing authority and appeals to the Transport Tribunal.)

(91 Section dealing with the powers of the Minister to make regulations under this Part of the Act.)

92—(1) In this Part of this Act and Schedule 9 thereto, unless the context otherwise requires—

"articulated combination" means a combination made up of—

(a) a motor vehicle which is so constructed that a trailer may by partial superimposition be attached to the vehicle in such a manner as to cause a substantial part of the weight of the trailer to be borne by the vehicle, and

(b) a trailer attached to it as aforesaid;

"authorised vehicle" means, in relation to an operator's licence, a vehicle authorised to be used thereunder, whether or not it is for the time being in use for a purpose for which an operator's licence is required and whether it is specified therein as so authorised or, being of a type so authorised subject to a maximum number, belongs to the holder of the licence or is in his possession under an agreement for hire-purchase, hire or loan;

"carriage of goods" includes haulage of goods;

"carrier's licence" means a licence granted under Part IV of the Act of 1960;

"contravention", in relation to any condition or provision, includes a failure to comply with the condition or provision, and "contravenes" shall be construed accordingly;

"driver" means, in relation to a trailer, the driver of the vehicle by which the trailer is drawn and "drive" shall be construed accordingly;

"goods" includes goods or burden of any description;

"goods vehicle" means, subject to subsection (5) of this section, a motor vehicle constructed or adapted for use for the carriage of goods, or a trailer so constructed or adapted;

"large goods vehicle" shall be construed in accordance with section 71 of this Act;

"operating centre" means, in relation to any vehicles, the base or centre from which the vehicles are, or are intended to be, normally used;

"prescribed" means prescribed by regulations;

"regulations" means regulations made by the Minister under this Part of this Act;

"subsidiary" means a subsidiary as defined by section 154 of the Companies Act 1948;

"vehicle combination" means a combination of goods vehicles made up of one or more motor vehicles and one or more trailers all of which are linked together when travelling;

and any expression not defined above which is also used in the Act of 1960 has the same meaning as in that Act.

(2) For the purposes of this Part of this Act, the driver of a vehicle, if it belongs to him or is in his possession under an agreement for hire, hire-purchase or loan, and in any other case the person whose servant or agent the driver is, shall be deemed to be the person using the vehicle; and references to using a vehicle shall be construed accordingly.

(3) In this Part of this Act references to directing that an operator's licence be curtailed are references to directing (with effect for the remainder of the duration of the licence or for any shorter period) all or any of the following, that is to say—

(a) that any one or more of the vehicles specified in the licence be removed therefrom;

(b) that the maximum number of trailers or of motor vehicles specified in the licence in pursuance of section 61(1)(*b*) or (*c*) of this Act be reduced;

(*c*) that the addition of authorised vehicles under the said section 61(1)(*c*) be no longer permitted.

(4) In this Part of this Act, references to the bankruptcy of a person shall, as respects Scotland, be construed as references to an award of sequestration having been made of his estate.

(5) In this Part of this Act and Schedule 9 thereto, references to goods vehicles do not include references to tramcars or trolley vehicles operated under statutory powers within the meaning of section 259 of the Act of 1960.

(6) Anything required or authorised by this Part of this Act to be done to or by a licensing authority by whom a licence or authorisation was granted may be done to or by any person for the time being acting as licensing authority for the area for which the first-mentioned authority was acting at the time of the granting of the licence or authorisation.

Abolition of carriers' licensing for certain vehicles

93—(1) Section 164 of the Act of 1960 (users of goods vehicles to hold carriers' licences) shall cease to apply to the use of any vehicle the unladen weight of which does not exceed thirty hundredweight, and any carrier's licence so far as it authorises the use of such a vehicle shall cease to have effect.

(2) The said section 164 shall not apply to the use of any vehicle for the use of which an operator's licence is required, unless that vehicle is a large goods vehicle.

(94 Section dealing with transitional provisions and amendments.)

PART VI

DRIVERS' HOURS

95—(1) This Part of this Act shall have effect with a view to securing the observance of proper hours of work by persons engaged in the carriage of passengers or goods by road and thereby protecting the public against the risks which arise in cases where the drivers of motor vehicles are suffering from fatigue.

(2) This Part of this Act applies to—

(*a*) passenger vehicles, that is to say—

(i) public service vehicles; and

(ii) motor vehicles (other than public service vehicles) constructed or adapted to carry more than twelve passengers;

(*b*) goods vehicles, that is to say—

(i) heavy locomotives, light locomotives, motor tractors and any motor vehicle so constructed that a trailer may by partial superimposition be attached to the vehicle in such a manner as to cause a substantial part of the weight of the trailer to be borne by the vehicle; and

(ii) motor vehicles (except those mentioned in paragraph (*a*) of this subsection) constructed or adapted to carry goods other than the effects of passengers.

(3) This Part of this Act applies to any such person as follows (in this Part of this Act referred to as "a driver"), that is to say—

(*a*) a person who drives a vehicle to which this Part of this Act applies in the course of his employment (in this Part of this Act referred to as "an employee-driver"); and

(*b*) a person who drives such a vehicle for the purposes of a trade or business carried on by him (in this Part of this Act referred to as "an owner-driver");

and in this Part of this Act references to driving by any person are references to his driving as aforesaid.

96—(1) Subject to the provisions of this section, a driver shall not on any working day drive a vehicle or vehicles to which this Part of this Act applies for periods amounting in the aggregate to more than ten hours.

(2) Subject to the provisions of this section, if on any working day a driver has been on duty for a period of, or for periods amounting in the aggregate to, five and a half hours and—

(*a*) there has not been during that period, or during or between any of those periods, an interval of not less than half an hour in which he was able to obtain rest and refreshment; and

(*b*) the end of that period, or of the last of those periods, does not mark the end of that working day,

there shall at the end of that period, or of the last of those periods, be such an interval as aforesaid.

(3) Subject to the provisions of this section, the working day of a driver—

(*a*) except where paragraph (*b*) or (*c*) of this subsection applies, shall not exceed eleven hours;

(*b*) if during that day he is off duty for a period which is, or periods which taken together are, not less than the time by which his working day exceeds eleven hours, shall not exceed twelve and a half hours;

(*c*) if during that day—

(i) all the time when he is driving vehicles to which this Part of this Act applies is spent in driving one or more express carriages or contract carriages; and

(ii) he is able for a period of not less than four hours to obtain rest and refreshment,

shall not exceed fourteen hours.

(4) Subject to the provisions of this section, there shall be, between any two successive working days of a driver, an interval for rest which—

(*a*) subject to paragraph (*b*) of this subsection, shall not be of less than eleven hours;

(*b*) if during both those days all or the greater part of the time when he is driving vehicles to which this Part of this Act applies is spent in driving one or more passenger vehicles, may, on one

183

occasion in each working week, be of less than eleven hours but not of less than nine and a half hours; and for the purposes of this Part of this Act a period of time shall not be treated, in the case of an employee-driver, as not being an interval for rest by reason only that he may be called upon to report for duty if required.

(5) Subject to the provisions of this section a driver shall not be on duty in any working week for periods amounting in the aggregate to more than sixty hours.

(6) Subject to the provisions of this section, there shall be, in the case of each working week of a driver, a period of not less than twenty-four hours for which he is off duty, being a period either falling wholly in that week or beginning in that week and ending in the next week; but—

(a) where the requirements of the foregoing provisions of this subsection have been satisfied in the case of any week by reference to a period ending in the next week, no part of that period (except any part after the expiration of the first twenty-four hours of it) shall be taken into account for the purpose of satisfying those requirements in the case of the next week; and

(b) those requirements need not be satisfied in the case of any working week of a driver who on each working day falling wholly or partly in that week drives one or more stage carriages if that week is immediately preceded by a week in the case of which those requirements have been satisfied as respects that driver or during which he has not at any time been on duty.

(7) If in the case of the working week of any driver the following requirement is satisfied, that is to say, that, in each of the periods of twenty-four hours beginning at midnight which make up that week, the driver does not drive a vehicle to which this Part of this Act applies for a period of, or periods amounting in the aggregate to, more than four hours, the foregoing provisions of this section shall not apply to him in that week, except that the provisions of subsections (1), (2) and (3) shall nevertheless have effect in relation to the whole of any working day falling partly in that week and partly in a working week in the case of which that requirement is not satisfied.

(8) If on any working day a driver does not drive any vehicle to which this Part of this Act applies—

(a) subsections (2) and (3) of this section shall not apply to that day, and

(b) the period or periods of duty attributable to that day for the purposes of subsection (5) of this section shall, if amounting to more than eleven hours, be treated as amounting to eleven hours only.

(9) For the purposes of subsections (1) and (7) of this section no account shall be taken of any time spent driving a vehicle elsewhere than on a road if the vehicle is being so driven in the course of operations of agriculture or forestry.

(10) For the purpose of enabling drivers to deal with cases of emergency or otherwise to meet a special need, the Minister may by regulations—

    (*a*) create exemptions from all or any of the requirements of sub-sections (1) to (6) of this section in such cases and subject to such conditions as may be specified in the regulations;

    (*b*) empower the traffic commissioners or licensing authority for any area, subject to the provisions of the regulations—

        (i) to dispense with the observance of all or any of those requirements (either generally or in such circumstances or to such extent as the commissioners or authority think fit) in any particular case for which provision is not made under paragraph (*a*) of this subsection;

        (ii) to grant a certificate (which, for the purposes of any proceedings under this Part of this Act, shall be conclusive evidence of the facts therein stated) that any particular case falls or fell within any exemption created under the said paragraph (*a*);

and regulations under this subsection may enable any dispensation under paragraph (*b*)(i) of this subsection to be granted retrospectively and provide for a document purporting to be a certificate granted by virtue of paragraph (*b*)(ii) of this subsection to be accepted in evidence without further proof.

(11) If any of the requirements of subsections (1) to (6) of this section, or any condition having effect by virtue of regulations made under sub-section (10) thereof, is contravened in the case of any driver—

    (*a*) that driver; and

    (*b*) any other person (being that driver's employer or a person to whose orders that driver was subject) who caused or permitted the contravention,

shall be liable on summary conviction to a fine not exceeding £200; but a person shall not be liable to be convicted under this subsection if he proves to the court—

    (i) that the contravention was due to unavoidable delay in the completion of a journey arising out of circumstances which he could not reasonably have foreseen; or

    (ii) in the case of a person charged under paragraph (*b*) of this subsection, that the contravention was due to the fact that the driver had for any particular period or periods driven or been on duty otherwise than in the employment of that person or, as the case may be, otherwise than in the employment in which he is subject to the orders of that person, and that the person charged was not, and could not reasonably have become, aware of that fact.

(12) The Minister may by order—

    (*a*) direct that subsection (1) of this section shall have effect with the substitution for the reference to ten hours of a reference to nine hours, either generally or with such exceptions as may be specified in the order;

    (*b*) direct that paragraph (*a*) of subsection (3) of this section shall have effect with the substitution for the reference to eleven hours of a reference to any shorter period, or remove, modify or add to the provisions of that subsection containing exceptions to the said paragraph (*a*);

(*c*) remove, modify or add to any of the requirements of subsections (2), (4), (5) or (6) of this section or any of the exemptions provided for by subsections (7), (8) and (9) thereof;

and any order under this subsection may contain such transitional and supplementary provisions as the Minister thinks necessary or expedient, including provisions amending any definition in section 103 of this Act which is relevant to any of the provisions affected by the order.

97—(1) Subject to the provisions of this section, no driver shall drive a vehicle to which this Part of this Act applies unless—

(*a*) there is installed in the vehicle in the prescribed place and manner equipment for recording information as to the use of the vehicle, being equipment of such type or design as may be prescribed or approved by the Minister for the purposes of this section; and

(*b*) that equipment is in working order.

(2) Subsection (1) of this section shall not apply to—

(*a*) a small goods vehicle as defined in section 103(6) of this Act; or

(*b*) a vehicle of any class exempted from that subsection by regulations made by the Minister;

and paragraph (*b*) of that subsection shall not apply in such cases as may be specified by regulations made by the Minister.

(3) The Minister may make regulations—

(*a*) imposing on the owner and driver of any vehicle in which equipment is installed for the purposes of this section, and the employer of an employee-driver, duties—

(i) as to the working of the equipment and for preventing misuse thereof;

(ii) as to any keys or other appliances used in connection with the equipment, including the keeping and preservation of records in connection with such keys or appliances;

(*b*) imposing on the owner of any vehicle in which equipment is installed for the purposes of this section duties as to the preservation of any records produced by means of the equipment.

(4) Any person who—

(*a*) contravenes subsection (1) of this section; or

(*b*) being the employer of any other person, or a person to whose orders any other person is subject, causes or permits that other person to contravene that sub-section; or

(*c*) contravenes any regulations made under subsection (3) of this section,

shall be liable on summary conviction to a fine not exceeding £200; but a person shall not be liable to be convicted by virtue of paragraph (*a*) or (*b*) of this subsection by reason of a contravention of subsection (1)(*b*) of this section if he proves to the court that the equipment in the vehicle in question ceased to be in working order in the course of a journey being undertaken by that vehicle, that neither he nor (if a different person) the

186

EXTRACTS FROM THE TRANSPORT ACT

driver of the vehicle was responsible for the equipment ceasing to be in working order and that the journey was not continued after it had become reasonably practicable in all the circumstances for the equipment to be restored to working order.

(5) A record produced by means of equipment installed for the purposes of this section in any vehicle shall, in any proceedings under this Part of this Act, be evidence of the matters appearing from the record.

98—(1) The Minister may make regulations—

(a) for requiring drivers to keep, and employers of employee-drivers to cause to be kept, in such books as may be specified in the regulations records with respect to such matters relevant to the enforcement of this Part of this Act as may be so specified; and

(b) for requiring owner-drivers and the employers of employee-drivers to maintain such registers as may be so specified with respect to any such books as aforesaid which are in their possession or in that of any employee-drivers in their employment.

(2) Regulations under this section may contain such supplementary and incidental provisions as the Minister thinks necessary or expedient, including in particular provisions—

(a) specifying the person or persons from whom books and registers required for the purposes of the regulations are to be obtained and, if provision is made for them to be obtained from the Minister, charging a fee for their issue by him (which shall be payable into the Consolidated Fund);

(b) as to the form and manner of making of entries in such books and registers;

(c) as to the issue by and return to the employers of employee-drivers of books required to be kept by the latter for the purposes of the regulations;

(d) requiring any book in current use for the purposes of the regulations to be carried on, or by the driver of, any vehicle, as to the preservation of any books and registers used for those purposes, and otherwise as to the manner in which those books and registers are to be dealt with;

(e) for exemptions from all or any of the requirements of the regulations in respect of drivers of small goods vehicles as defined in section 103(6) of this Act and for other exemptions from all or any of those requirements.

(3) Subject to the provisions of any regulations made by the Minister, the traffic commissioners or licensing authority for any area may dispense with the observance by any employee-driver of his employer, or by any owner-driver, of any requirement imposed under this section, either generally or in such circumstances or to such extent as the commissioners or authority think fit, but the traffic commissioners or licensing authority shall not grant such a dispensation unless satisfied that it is not reasonably practicable for the requirement dispensed with to be observed.

(4) Any person who contravenes any regulations made under this section shall be liable on summary conviction to a fine not exceeding

£200; but the employer of an employee-driver shall not be liable to be convicted under this subsection by reason of contravening any such regulation whereby he is required to cause any records to be kept if he proves to the court that he has given proper instructions to his employees with respect to the keeping of the records and has from time to time taken reasonable steps to secure that those instructions are being carried out.

(5) Any entry made by an employee-driver for the purposes of regulations under this section shall, in any proceedings under this Part of this Act, be admissible in evidence against his employer.

99—(1) An officer may, on production if so required of his authority, require any person to produce, and permit him to inspect and copy—

(a) any book or register which that person is required by regulations under section 98 of this Act to carry or have in his possession for the purpose of making in it any entry required by those regulations or which is required under those regulations to be carried on any vehicle of which that person is the driver;

(b) any record, book or register which that person is required by regulations under section 97 or 98 of this Act to preserve;

(c) if that person is the owner of a vehicle to which this Part of this Act applies, any other document of that person which the officer may reasonably require to inspect for the purpose of ascertaining whether the provisions of this Part of this Act or of regulations made thereunder have been complied with;

and that record, book, register or document shall, if the officer so requires by notice in writing served on that person, be produced at the office of the traffic commissioners or licensing authority specified in the notice within such time (not being less than ten days) from the service of the notice as may be so specified.

(2) An officer may, on production if so required of his authority—

(a) at any time, enter any vehicle to which this Part of this Act applies and inspect that vehicle and any equipment installed in it for the purposes of section 97 of this Act and inspect and copy any record on the vehicle which has been produced by means of that equipment;

(b) at any time which is reasonable having regard to the circumstances of the case, enter any premises on which he has reason to believe that such a vehicle is kept or that any such records, books, registers or other documents as are mentioned in subsection (1) of this section are to be found, and inspect any such vehicle, and inspect and copy any such record, book, register or document, which he finds there.

(3) For the purpose of exercising his powers under subsection (2)(a) and, in respect of a document carried on, or by the driver of, a vehicle, under subsection (1)(a) of this section, an officer may detain the vehicle in question during such time as is required for the exercise of that power.

(4) Any person who—

(a) fails to comply with any requirement under subsection (1) of this section; or

(*b*) obstructs an officer in the exercise of his powers under subsection (2) or (3) of this section,
shall be liable on summary conviction to a fine not exceeding £100.

(5) Any person who makes, or causes to be made, any such record as is mentioned in section 97 of this Act or any entry in a book or register kept for the purposes of regulations under section 98 thereof which he knows to be false or, with intent to deceive, alters or causes to be altered any such record or entry shall be liable—

    (*a*) on summary conviction, to a fine not exceeding £200;

    (*b*) on conviction on indictment, to imprisonment for a term not exceeding two years.

(6) If an officer has reason to believe that an offence under subsection (5) of this section has been committed in respect of any record or document inspected by him under this section, he may seize that record or document; and where a record or document is seized as aforesaid and within six months of the date on which it was seized no person has been charged since that date with an offence in relation to that record or document under that subsection and the record or document has not been returned to the person from whom it was taken, a magistrate's court shall, on an application made for the purpose by that person or by an officer, make such order respecting the disposal of the record or document and award such costs as the justice of the case may require.

(7) Any proceedings in Scotland under subsection (6) of this section shall be taken by way of summary application in the sheriff court; and in the application of that subsection to Scotland references to costs shall be construed as references to expenses.

(8) In this section "officer" means a certifying officer appointed under Part III of the Act of 1960, a public service vehicle examiner, an examiner appointed under Part IV of that Act and any person authorised for the purposes of this section by the traffic commissioners or licensing authority for any area.

(9) The powers conferred by this section on an officer as defined in subsection (8) of this section shall be exercisable also by a police constable, who shall not, if wearing uniform, be required to produce any authority.

(10) In this section references to the inspection and copying of any record produced by means of equipment installed for the purposes of section 97 of this Act in a vehicle include references to the application to the record of any process for eliciting the information recorded thereby and to taking down the information elicited from it.

(**100** Section dealing with the power of the Minister to give effect to international arrangements.)

(**101** Section dealing with the procedure for making regulations under Part VI of the Act.)

(**102** Section dealing with the application of Part VI of the Act to vehicles moved by the Crown, the police and the fire brigade.)

    103—(1) In this Part of this Act—

    "agriculture" has the meaning assigned by section 109(3) of the

Agriculture Act 1947 or, in relation to Scotland, section 86(3) of the Agriculture (Scotland) Act 1948;

"driver," "employee-driver" and "owner-driver" have the meaning assigned by section 95(3) of this Act;

"employer," in relation to an employee-driver, means the employer of that driver in the employment by virtue of which that driver is an employee-driver;

"licensing authority" has the same meaning as in Part V of this Act;

"prescribed" means prescribed by regulations made by the Minister;

"working day," in relation to any driver, means—

> (a) any period during which he is on duty and which does not fall to be aggregated with any other such period by virtue of paragraph (b) of this definition; and

> (b) where a period during which he is on duty is not followed by an interval for rest of not less than eleven hours of (where permitted by virtue of section 96(4)(b) of this Act) of not less than nine and a half hours, the aggregate of that period and each successive such period until there is such an interval as aforesaid, together with any interval or intervals between periods so aggregated;

"working week" means, subject to subsection (5) of this section, a week beginning at midnight between Saturday and Sunday;

and any expression not defined above which is also used in the Act of 1960 has the same meaning as in that Act.

(2) For the purposes of this Part of this Act a director of a company shall be deemed to be employed by it.

(3) In this Part of this Act references to a person driving a vehicle are references to his being at the driving controls of the vehicle for the purpose of controlling its movement, whether it is in motion or is stationary with the engine running.

(4) In this Part of this Act references to a driver being on duty are references—

> (a) in the case of an employee-driver, to his being on duty (whether for the purpose of driving a vehicle to which this Part of this Act applies or for other purposes) in the employment by virtue of which he is an employee-driver, or in any other employment under the person who is his employer in the first-mentioned employment; and

> (b) in the case of an owner-driver, to his driving a vehicle to which this Part of this Act applies for the purposes of a trade or business carried on by him or being otherwise engaged in work for the purposes of that trade or business, being work in connection with such a vehicle or the load carried thereby.

(5) The traffic commissioners or licensing authority for any area may, on the application of an owner-driver or of the employer of an employee-driver, from time to time direct that a week beginning at midnight between two days other than Saturday and Sunday shall be, or be deemed to have been, a working week in relation to that owner-driver or employee-driver;

but where by virtue of any such direction a new working week begins before the expiration of a previous working week then, without prejudice to the application of the provisions of this Part of this Act in relation to the new working week, those provisions shall continue to apply in relation to the previous working week until its expiration.

(6) In sections 97(2)(*a*) and 98(2)(*e*) of this Act "a small goods vehicle" means a goods vehicle which has a plated weight of the prescribed description not exceeding three and a half tons or (not having a plated weight) has an unladen weight not exceeding thirty hundredweight; but the Minister may by regulations direct that the foregoing provisions of this subsection shall have effect, in relation to either or both of those sections—

(*a*) with the substitution for either of the weights there specified or such other weight as may be specified in the regulations;

(*b*) with the substitution for either of those weights or for any other weight for the time being specified as aforesaid of a weight expressed in terms of the metric system, being a weight which is equivalent to that for which it is substituted or does not differ from it by more than five per cent thereof.

(7) Without prejudice to any jurisdiction of any court under any other enactment, proceedings for an offence under this Part of this Act may be commenced in any court having jurisdiction in the place where the person charged with the offence is for the time being.

(8) The enactments specified in Schedule 11 to this Act shall have effect subject to the amendments there specified.

(9) Any order made under section 166(2) of this Act appointing a day for the purposes of any of the provisions of this Part of this Act may contain such transitional provision as the Minister thinks necessary or expedient as respects the application of any particular provision of this Part of this Act to a working week or working day falling partly before and partly after the date on which that provision comes into operation.

Index

196